Preaching, Planning, & Plumbing

*The Implications of Bivocational Ministry
For the Church and for You–
Discovering God's Call to Service and Joy*

Steve Clapp, Ron Finney, and Angela Zimmerman

Christian Community
Resources

**A Joint Project Of
The Brethren Academy and Christian Community**

Preaching, Planning, and Plumbing
The Implications of Bivocational Ministry for the Church and for You–Discovering God's Call to Service and Joy

By Steve Clapp, Ron Finney, and Angela Zimmerman

Cover design and illustrations by Herb Eveland. Our thanks to Evangel Press for their production of this book.

ISBN 1-893270-02-5

Manufactured in the United States of America

*This book is dedicated to the millions of
committed people who regularly utilize
their spiritual gifts in Christ's service
as full-time ministers, bivocational ministers,
and church members.
Many of these people give sacrificially
of their time and material resources
with little formal recognition.
All of us are called to the ministry,
to be Christ's presence to a world in need.*

*"For just as the body is one
and has many members,
and all the members of the body,
though many, are one body,
so it is with Christ.*

*For in the one Spirit
we were all baptized into one body–
Jews or Greeks, slave or free–
and we were all made
to drink of one Spirit."*

1 Corinthians 12:12-13

Contents

Many men and women serving the church as pastor have an additional occupation or vocation.

Introduction

We hope people from many different backgrounds will be reading this introduction and the pages which follow. This book is about ministry–not only the ministry of persons who have been trained and licensed or ordained for set-apart work but also the ministry of all people who are part of the body of Christ.

The preparation of this book started with a study of bivocational ministry–a look at those persons who serve as pastors of churches but who have an additional vocation or occupation. Some, as the book title suggests, are plumbers; others are teachers, mail carriers, physicians, real estate agents, car dealers, lawyers, and bankers. The variety of additional occupations, in fact, is much greater than we had anticipated. The bivocational minister generally draws financial support from both positions, though sometimes all the support comes from the non-ministry position. Because these pastors have one foot in the church and another in the secular world, their work has much to teach us about the ministry to which all of us are called as followers of Christ.

In the process of learning more about bivocational ministry, we repeatedly found ourselves dealing with questions like:

- What is ministry? What do we really mean by "the priesthood of all believers," a concept accepted by most mainline Protestant and Anabaptist churches?

- What does bivocational ministry teach us both about the set-apart ministry and about the ministry to which all people are called?

- How can people be helped to better identify and understand the spiritual gifts which they have received and determine how to use them in Christ's service?

This book will be of interest to:

- Individual church members and clergy who are seeking to better understand the ministry to which they are called.

- Executives and seminary faculty in most Protestant and Anabaptist denominations.

- Study groups including Sunday school classes, church boards, seminary classes, regional judicatory groups responsible for ministry, and others. A discussion guide can be found at the back of the book.

Our survey research on bivocational ministry was done within the Church of the Brethren. Many people reading this book, however, will not be members of the Church of the Brethren and may know very little about the denomination. It is a relatively small denomination with a membership under 150,000, but its heritage is one of the oldest in the United States. The Church of the Brethren began in Schwarzenau, Germany, in 1708; and it is one of the three historic peace churches (along with the Mennonites and the Friends).

The denomination has extensive peace and justice ministries

and is a continuing participant in the work of the World Council of Churches and the National Council of Churches. It is not a strongly doctrinal denomination, and its members reflect a broad range of theological views. Church of the Brethren congregations routinely work cooperatively with the United Methodist Church, the Disciples of Christ, the American Baptist Church, the United Church of Christ, the Presbyterian Church, the African Methodist Episcopal Church, and other mainline Protestant churches as well as with the Mennonites and Friends.

The members of the Church of the Brethren are distributed in slightly less than eleven hundred congregations, 72% of which have fewer than 150 members. As a result, supporting a full-time minister is beyond the present financial resources of many congregations; and bivocational ministers have been viewed as a necessity.

The service of bivocational ministers, however, does not need to be limited to small congregations. Many large congregations of many different denominations have a significant need for more clergy to carry out specialized ministries, and bivocational ministry offers valuable potential for such churches.

This book starts with the question "What Is Ministry?" and provides guidance in determining the answer to that question not only for the church as an institution but for each of us as individuals. We urge you to read the book with care, to take seriously the spiritual gifts inventory which appears in the second chapter, and to talk about the book with others.

We extend appreciation to the many people who helped us with this book by completing surveys on bivocational ministry and by helping refine a spiritual gifts process. This book would not have been possible without the encouragement of Bethany Theological Seminary and the Council of District Executives of the Church of the Brethren.

We anticipate offering other resources on this topic, and we would be delighted to hear about your experiences with this book. Ron Finney can be contacted at:

The Brethren Academy
Bethany Theological Seminary
615 National Road West
Richmond, Indiana 47374

Steve Clapp and Angela Zimmerman can be contacted at:

Christian Community
6404 S. Calhoun Street
Fort Wayne, Indiana 46807

Steve, Ron, and Angela

What does ministry mean for you?

- Using gifts and abilities in God's service?

- Reaching out in the name of Christ?

- Preaching?

- Teaching?

- Planning the church's program?

- Raising funds for the church?

- Visiting the sick?

- Working for peace and justice?

- Inviting others to commit their
  lives to Christ and become involved
  in the church?

- Having a seminary degree?

- Being committed to Christ's work
  twenty-four hours a day?

All of us have a ministry as part of the body of Christ.

Chapter One
What Is Ministry?

*Indeed, the body does not consist of one
member but of many. If the foot would say,
"Because I am not a hand, I do not belong to
the body," that would not make it any less a
part of the body.*

1 Corinthians 12:14-15

Michael was relieved when he hung up the telephone. When he had answered the phone thirty minutes earlier, at 10:30 p.m., he had anticipated that the call would bring news of Martha's death. The physicians had decided to discontinue the chemotherapy and hadn't been optimistic she would make it through the week. One person had recently called Martha "the Grandmother of the whole congregation," and Michael supposed that was an accurate description. He had grown very fond of her during his five years as pastor of St. Mark's; and while he recognized that death would be a relief from suffering for her, his own life would feel diminished by her death just as it had felt enriched by her life.

But the call hadn't been about Martha. The call had come from Beth, the church's music director. Beth had turned in her resignation five days earlier and said that she was planning to accept a position with another congregation, which would pay her over fifty percent more than St. Mark's had. Beth had so much energy and passion for her work that her loss would have been a major one to the church. As Michael had visited with her the day of her resignation, he had realized that the church's failure to give her any financial increase for the past three years had caused her to feel unappreciated and taken advantage of. She had acted like the money wasn't important to her because the church's budget had been tight. No one, including Michael, had thought about the message Beth might be receiving from the failure to extend regular increases.

She had not actually accepted the other position at the time of her resignation, so Michael had asked her to give him a few days to talk with people about her compensation package. She had felt awkward but had reluctantly agreed to postpone accepting the new position. He had called an emergency meeting of the personnel committee and then of the church board, and they had revised her salary and benefit package significantly. The chairperson of the church board had gone to her home to express the church's strong desire for her to continue. The late night phone call had been Beth sharing her decision to stay at the church.

Thank you, God, Michael silently prayed. Dealing with Beth's situation had consumed most of the week. He knew it was important to the church and to Beth, but it had sure put him behind on almost everything else. He reflected, as he had on many other occasions, that there was certainly a lot more to the practice of ministry than he had realized while a seminary student.

Laura, an active layperson in a congregation five hundred miles away from the one Michael served, also hung up the phone at 11 p.m. with considerable relief. She was a human resources executive with a large company and had recently taken a significant chance. Six months earlier her company had been planning to fire an employee who had been with the organization for fifteen years. He deserved dismissal all right; he had developed a chronic habit of coming into work late because of a drinking problem.

As Laura had started to sign off on the termination papers, her mind had flashed to what she had read during her devotions that morning: "Sometimes we are given the opportunity to help destroy a life or to help turn a life around. Those are the times when we need to remember what Christ has done for us." It had felt to Laura as though those words were meant just for her that day. The employee had a year of bad work history, but his record for the fourteen previous years had been excellent. Couldn't this life be redeemed?

She spoke to the company nurse about the alcohol problem; visited with the employee's manager; and finally called the employee into her office for a frank conversation. When the employee had talked about feeling like a failure to everyone, including God, Laura had shared her confidence that Christ could help anyone find new life.

Then she had persuaded the manager to give the employee another chance on the condition that the employee begin a rehabilitation program which would be paid for by the company. A vice president had to approve the rehabilitation program, and Laura knew she put a lot on the line in asking for that to happen.

The phone call she had received that evening had been from the vice president, who had called to say that he had run into the employee at a restaurant that evening and had visited with him. Laura cringed inwardly, assuming that the phone call so late at night could only mean that the employee had been drinking and that the vice president was unhappy about the bad investment. Instead, it turned out that the vice president was very impressed by the turn-around that the employee had made in his life. The employee had said that Laura still having confidence in him had made all the difference, and the vice president had called to tell her that. Laura said a prayer of thanksgiving that life was so much better for the employee and that her own position in the company had been strengthened rather than jeopardized by the chance she had taken.

Five hundred miles in another direction, John hung up his phone at 11 p.m. with a strong sense of satisfaction. He worked as an English teacher in a local high school and was also the pastor of a relatively small congregation. The chairperson of the church's financial campaign had called to tell John that the results of the campaign had been calculated and that the members had made financial commitments which exceeded the initial budget that the board had prepared. The morale of the congregation was very high, and it would be possible for them to do the renovation work that was needed in the Sunday school classrooms. The chairperson had especially wanted to express his appreciation for the stewardship education program which John had helped initiate and which seemed to have played a major role in raising the giving level of the congregation.

Juggling the secular position and the church position at times left John feeling drained and wondering if he was giving his best performance either place. Yet both attendance and giving had improved over the past year in the church; and the strong financial campaign was further confirmation that people felt good about what was happening. The week had also been a good one at school, with two difficult students responding well to John's leadership. John felt as though his life had been richly blessed.

The three people just described each have significant gifts and abilities which they are using in the service of Christ. In terms of church organization or polity, they represent three different approaches to ministry:

1. Michael in the full-time, set apart ministry.
2. Laura as a layperson with no ministerial training but seeking to act on her faith in the midst of her daily work.
3. John in both a secular position and a church position.

John is a bivocational pastor. The phrase bivocational ministry, as used in this book, refers to a situation in which a pastor has an additional vocation or occupation. The bivocational minister generally draws financial support from both positions, though sometimes all the support comes from a non-ministry position.

The person in bivocational ministry is in a unique role, and our desire to understand that role resulted in the book which you hold in your hands. As the three of us worked cooperatively with others to understand bivocational ministry, we found ourselves repeatedly confronting the basic question: What is ministry?

A Three-Tiered View

Protestant and Anabaptist congregations affirm a view of the church which includes the concept of "the priesthood of all believers." We believe that all people are called to ministry and that all people have received gifts from God for use in ministry. While Roman Catholics would not so readily use the words "priesthood of all believers," the concept of personal ministry has gained in importance in Catholic churches. **The word ministry is sometimes used in a narrowly defined sense to designate a person trained and employed by the church for set-apart work, but almost all denominations also see ministry as service in Christ's name and as work for which the entire church has responsibility.**

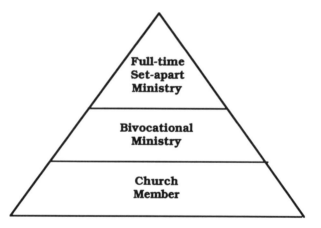

Although most of us would not put it so crassly, the reality is that we are often tempted to see ministry as a three-tiered kind of enterprise. Those at the top are the full-time, seminary trained, set-apart clergy. Bivocational ministers are the next level, followed by laypersons in the congregation.

When we think about bivocational ministry, we often do so in economic terms. The inability of a congregation to pay the salary and benefits of a full-time pastor is generally the major factor in the decision to call as minister a person with another source of income. Those who choose to work as bivocational ministers often have economic factors of their own influencing that choice:

- They may have experienced a call to ministry later in life but feel unable to fully leave the secular occupation because of a high income level, retirement benefits, or enjoyment of the field.

- They may have started work as a full-time minister but have sought additional employment when a church which would pay a full-time salary could not be found or when they wanted to continue pastoring a church with a declining financial base.

- They may have consciously chosen to maintain a secular job in order to serve congregations too small to afford a full-time pastor.

But while financial factors are clearly at work among bivocational clergy, our study made it clear that the vast majority feel a genuine call to bivocational ministry. Economics are not the only factor involved.

Michael certainly spends a greater portion of his day doing things most of us associate with the practice of ministry than either John or Laura. Some of those activities, like working out a different salary and benefit package in order to retain a music director, are important but don't seem particularly unique to the set-apart ministry. The counseling and hospital visitation which Michael has done with Martha seem more clearly in the province of ministry, but there are congregations in which almost all hospital and shut-in visitation is carried out by lay volunteers.

Beth, the music director, may well have felt that what Michael did on her behalf was a very important ministry, and it's quite possible that no one else could have achieved so much in a five day period of time. But Laura's ministry of compassion to the employee with the drinking problem was also significant. If Laura had not been in her position, the employee would certainly have been terminated and might not have become involved in such an effective rehabilitation program.

The reality is that the lines separating what Michael, Laura, and John do are not so clear as they may first appear. Certainly the unofficial three-tiered view which we often accept is an unfair one to all three persons. It would be healthier to think of their ministries being different but on the same level of call:

Full-Time Set-Apart Ministry	Bivocational Ministry	Church Members' Ministry

The Free Ministry Heritage

In the Church of the Brethren heritage, all people are considered ministers; but some are called out for ordination and the special leadership roles which accompany that designation and training. Until the early 1920s, "free ministry" was the tradition in the Church of the Brethren. Ministers were expected to provide their own support. Because it was difficult for one person to lead a congregation in addition to paid work, this often meant having several members help lead the congregation. Churches were careful not to elevate ministers above others in the congregation. The free ministry obviously has strong support in Scripture with early church leaders continuing to work at secular trades to provide income. Free ministry has always, in a sense, been bivocational. Some prefer the designation "plural, non-salaried ministry" or "self-supporting ministry" to "free ministry."

Although free ministry continues in several congregations in the denomination, there has been considerable growth since the 1920s in the percentage of churches which pay their ministers and in the number of clergy who work full-time for the church and derive all their financial support from that pastoral work. Many congregations, however, cannot afford a full-time pastor. Those congregations are served in a variety of ways: by being linked with one or more other churches to share the support of a pastor; by being served through a student pastor; by being served by a retired person working as pastor; or by being served by a bivocational pastor. Both student pastors and retired persons working as pastors can be viewed as bivocational in some respects.

Most denominations face the problem of some congregations being too small to afford full-time pastoral leadership. While the free ministry or plural, non-salaried ministry is not a common approach in most denominations, the other options used by the Church of the Brethren are held in common with many other churches such as the United Methodist Church, American Baptist Churches, the Presbyterian Church, and the Disciples of Christ.

As suggested before, the issues are not all economic. The Church of the Brethren has some large congregations which are served by plural, non-salaried ministers, and those congregations are thriving. These are churches which can certainly afford full-time pastoral staff, but they choose to continue the free ministry model. Financial resources which would otherwise go to the salary and benefits of staff members can be utilized for service and outreach. Members of such churches may feel a greater commitment to participation in the church's ministry because no one is being hired to do so. When the pastoral staff members receive no salary, there is room for a higher level of expectation of the participation of all church members.

Those who work as free ministers or as plural, non-salaried ministers are at least bivocational to the extent that they must have some source of financial support since they are not paid by the congregation. Many of those persons have secular occupations, and some are retired. All of them feel a call to serve the church.

The Money and the Members Can Be Found

There is a danger of some congregations determining too quickly that a full-time, salaried pastor is beyond their financial resources. Some strategies have the potential for expanding the available resources for a congregation:

1. The development of a comprehensive program of services and hospitality which will attract new people to the life of the church, expanding both personnel and financial resources.

2. The development of an evangelism program which trains members to share their faith with others and to bring new people into the life of the church.

3. The development of a stewardship program which expands the giving capacity of members from the typical average of 2%–3% of personal income to the 10% standard of the tithe, thus making available greater financial resources.

Obviously the implementation of those strategies involves an enormous amount of work and requires both commitment and enthusiasm. The specific strategies for accomplishing those strategies goes beyond the scope of this book.

There are many small congregations which, for a variety of reasons including demographic limitations, are not likely to make significant increases in their membership size or their giving level. There will always be small churches with ministries to be carried out that are just as important as those of much larger congregations.

The approaches to ministry discussed in this book can help not only small, often struggling congregations but can also result in new energy and enthusiasm for larger congregations. Whose job is ministry? It's the job of all of us who claim to be disciples of Christ. And that ministry involves not only what we do in the church but also what we do in the community. We are to be Christ's presence in our homes, our neighborhoods, and in our secular employment as well as in the work we do through the congregation.

In this chapter, we invite you to spend some time filling out a form: a spiritual gift assessment to be used as a guide in thinking about the ministries to which Christ may be calling you.

Chapter Two
Gifts for Ministry

Are all apostles? Are all prophets? Are all teachers?
Do all work miracles? Do all possess gifts of healing?
Do all speak in tongues? Do all interpret? But strive
for the greater gifts. And I will show you a still more
excellent way.

1 Corinthians 12:29-31

This chapter includes an
exercise designed to help
you assess your own spiritual
gifts. You can complete the
exercise at this time, or you
can come back to it when
you read Chapter Six,
"What Is Your Ministry?"

Spiritual Gifts Overview

Protestant and Anabaptist traditions affirm not only the
concept of the priesthood of all believers but also the belief that
God has given us gifts to be used in service to the church and to
others. Some people think of spiritual gifts narrowly like
speaking in tongues or having the gift of healing, but most
spiritual gifts are not spectacular or controversial.

An understanding of your spiritual gifts can be a significant
help in focusing your ministry in the most effective ways,

whether you are a full-time minister, a bivocational minister, or a church member. Most of us have between two and five spiritual gifts, and we should seek to maximize those gifts in our ministries and in our lives. That doesn't mean, of course, that we only work within the areas of our spiritual gifts. Every local church has numerous important tasks that must be done–whether someone feels gifted in each of those areas or not! To the extent that it is possible, however, people are more fulfilled and energized when they work in their areas of giftedness. That reality is true of laypersons in the church and also true of clergy. It's also true for those working in secular settings.

Spiritual gifts are not:

- acquired skills or natural abilities. Such skills and abilities are often used in the practice of spiritual gifts but are not the same thing. Cooking and cleaning, for example, are not themselves spiritual gifts but may help with the gift of hospitality.

- roles or offices (like being a pastor or the church treasurer).

- related only to the health and work of the church as an organization. We are part of the ministry of the overall body of Christ, which means that our gifts are to be used not only in relationship to the church as an organization but also in our homes, in our neighborhoods, and at places of secular employment. In the last chapter, it was clear that Laura used her spiritual gifts and her sense of call in her secular work.

- intended to be used for self-glory or in a way that divides the body of Christ. Spiritual gifts need to be held with true humility and thankfulness. The fact that one is especially gifted in an area does not mean that no one else should work in that area or that the opinions of others should not be respected.

- the same for everyone. Different people have different gifts. That's how the body of Christ works. No one person has all the gifts needed but by working together people find that the overall needs of the church can be met. There may be times, however, when a church in decline is missing some gifts which would be helpful.

Read chapter twelve in First Corinthians for a better understanding of the role that each person plays in the healthy functioning of the body of Christ.

- an excuse for neglecting areas of need. We should all practice acts of encouragement, for example, even though some are especially gifted in that area. All of us need to reach out to others, inviting them to be part of the Christian community, even if we do not personally possess the gift of evangelism.

- necessarily clearly revealed by any system of human design, including this one. Assessment systems can, however, be a significant aid to you in better understanding your spiritual gifts.

Spiritual gifts are:

- unmerited favors or gifts from God. We do not earn them or receive them as rewards for what we have done.

- an indicator of areas in which we should be working in the life of the church and in our secular work as well.

- able to be more fully developed by study and practice. A person with the gift of teaching, for example, will be a better teacher with training and careful preparation.

- meant to be used as part of the body of Christ–so that we work together in mutually beneficial ways not only in the institutional church but also in society as a whole.

- confirmed to us through prayer and through the feedback of the Christian community. We recommend, for example, that you have at least one other person complete an assessment form *about you* in addition to the one you complete. Seeing how another person experiences or observes your gifts will help in the assessment process.

As already indicated, there are many different systems for assessing spiritual gifts. The gifts described here are similar to those in several other spiritual gift assessment systems. They are organized here into three major categories:

1. Communication Gifts
2. Organization-Strengthening Gifts
3. Relationship Gifts

The Appendix provides information on another category of spiritual gifts which are less commonly found and not readily assessed by a system such as this one. That category includes the gifts of speaking in tongues and healing which are of value to the body of Christ when used in a supportive kind of way. They can also be divisive, especially when people place too much importance on them.

Four Communication Gifts

Prophecy: The God-given ability to share and interpret God's message and call to justice for the repentance, enrichment, or uplifting of the body of Christ and of persons and organizations outside of the church. This may be communicated through the written or the spoken word. Note that one may have the gift of prophecy without necessarily being an extremely skilled preacher. It's also possible to be a skilled preacher as a manifestation of the gift of teaching without having the gift of prophecy.   Some persons express the gift of prophecy in speaking directly to secular organizations or to society as a whole. Some large corporations have prophets in their midst who become a kind of "corporate conscience" which may make a tremendous difference in those organizations.

Teaching: The God-given ability to teach others how to understand Scripture, God, relationships, themselves, and the world in which we have been placed. While we especially think of this gift being utilized in the educational program and ministry of the church, it also finds expression in quality preaching. Those with the gift of teaching may also employ it in significant ways in secular school systems or anywhere there is opportunity to help others learn. In secular settings, of course, one must respect the diversity of beliefs and not impose the faith on others.

Artistic Expression: The God-given ability to share God's love through one or more art forms such as music, drama, poetry, painting, sculpturing, etc. We find evidence of people having this gift throughout the Old and the New Testaments. The expression of this gift is not limited to the life of the church as an organization.

Intercession: The God-given ability to live a life much of which is immersed in prayer for the needs of other people, the church, and the world. The communication is between the person and God, though it may become public in services of worship and other settings.

Four Organization-Strengthening Gifts

Administration: The God-given ability to understand organizations and to further the work of the body of Christ through efficiency, planning, and procedure. This gift is a great blessing to those with management responsibilities. While we especially think of the expression of this gift within the church, persons in secular employment may see administrative functions as an expression of a God-given gift, to be used for the sharing of God's love.

Craftsmanship: The God-given ability to create resources needed in the body of Christ (which can include carpentry, sewing, etc.).   People who are gifted in this area may also find great meaning in secular work which involves a high level of creativity in construction and design.

Generosity: The God-given ability to contribute money and material resources to the work of the body of Christ with a thankful heart. The fact that one has this gift does not automatically mean that one is wealthy, and the fact that one is wealthy does not mean that one necessarily possesses this gift. The work of the body of Christ is done not only through the institutional church but also through secular organizations, so support of worthy causes outside the church may also be an expression of this spiritual gift. People with this gift often have a high ability to cultivate generosity in others.

Service: The God-given ability to experience spiritual value in practical tasks which support the work of the church and help others. This is closely related to the gift of hospitality. People with this gift may also find great meaning in the service they offer at secular work and in community organizations.

Five Relationship Gifts

Counseling: The God-given ability to effectively listen to people and guide them in becoming more fulfilled spiritually, psychologically, and socially. People who are gifted in this area can find many opportunities to utilize and develop the gift in secular work as well as in the life of the church.

Encouragement: The God-given ability to support, encourage, and strengthen those who are suffering or who are going through a crisis in their faith or in their lives. As with counseling, there are many opportunities in the secular world to utilize this gift–in the home, in neighborhoods, in volunteer work, and in secular employment.

Evangelism: The God-given ability to share Christ's message with people who have no faith or who are unsure of their faith–so that they can move toward deeper relationships with Christ. While possessing this gift can obviously be a tremendous advantage for a pastor, there are many with the gift who choose to work in secular occupations because of the opportunities for involvement with people which those occupations bring.

Hospitality: The God-given ability to embrace people, including strangers, and to provide companionship, food, and shelter when needed. This is related to but not identical with the kind of biblical hospitality which we are all obligated to practice as part of the body of Christ. Many people with this gift find meaning working in the social services field or doing volunteer work with nonprofits which serve the homeless, the hungry, and the imprisoned.

Leadership: The God-given ability to identify and communicate a vision or mission and to direct people in making the vision or mission a reality. This is not the same as the gift of administration. The gift of leadership is very powerful and can be utilized in a wide range of occupations as well as in the church.

The Bible on Spiritual Gifts

As you are preparing to work through the spiritual gifts assessment process which follows, you may find it helpful to read some of the biblical references to spiritual gifts. For example:

- 1 Corinthians 12–14
- Romans 12
- Ephesians 4
- 1 Peter 4
- James 5:14-16 and 1 Timothy 2:1-2 (intercession)
- Other references to artistic expression and to craftsmanship are found in many Old Testament passages.

Variations in Spiritual Gifts Identified

Some systems of spiritual gifts take just one of the biblical passages shared above as a standard and include only those gifts which are explicitly named in that passage. Others broaden the concept considerably and may include as spiritual gifts celibacy, exorcism, and martyrdom. There do not seem to be many people eager to claim those gifts in our time!

While spiritual gifts are divine blessings, all systems of identifying and assessing spiritual gifts, as already mentioned, are human systems–with all the shortcomings that accompany everything else we do as human beings! The gifts included in the following inventory reflect the gifts identified by a substantial number of persons who have studied this field. The system is biblical, but it does include some contemporary terminology (such as "counseling" for those gifted at helping people in their quest for wholeness). There may well be spiritual gifts which are not reflected as such in Scripture or in any inventory system. Some people feel that "parenting" or "child raising" is a spiritual gift even though all of us who parent learn to cultivate our skills in that area.

Inventories like this one, the feedback of people who know you very well, and group discussions can be a help in clarifying gifts. The bottom line is that each person must prayerfully consider what spiritual gifts he or she has and how those should be used.

Completing the Assessments

You may wish to make one or more photocopies of the assessment which follows so that you can ask at least one friend or family member to complete it for you. Then you can compare those responses to your own.

It's best not to reflect at great length on the answers to individual items in the assessment. Simply move through, giving your first inclination as a response in most instances.

When completed, transfer the numerical responses to the overview or summary sheet which follows the assessment items. By totaling those in the indicated columns, you'll have weighted responses on the thirteen spiritual gifts. The three or four highest scores are most likely spiritual gifts for you. Some people, however, may find only one or two which clearly stand out from the others in terms of score; and some may find as many as six or seven which have high scores.

Have at least one person who knows you extremely well complete the items for you, and transfer the numerical scores to the overview or summary sheet provided. Obviously there are some items which require that the friend or associate make educated estimates concerning your impact on other people or how you feel about certain experiences. Those estimates, however, reflect something of how you come across to others and are valuable feedback.

It's important that you clearly communicate to anyone who completes the assessment for you that you want that person's honest feedback. Ideal persons to complete the form for you would include a spouse, a person at your place of work who has known you for two or more years, a person who has been a friend for many years, or an active lay person or staff member in the church who has worked with you for two or more years. You may decide to have three or four people complete the assessment for you. Make as many copies as you need for that purpose.

Compare the results of the assessment of other persons with your own. Where the assessments are essentially in agreement, you have added confirmation of the validity of those spiritual gifts. If there are spiritual gifts where you and a person doing the friend or associate assessment are not in agreement, you want to put the final confidence in your own assessment. The fact that you are not in agreement, however, may cause you to look again at your own responses to the items used to produce the weighted score for that spiritual gift (simply follow the numbers in the column on the overview sheet for that gift). You might determine that your initial responses were too high or too low based on the additional feedback.

As you reflect and pray on the assessment results, you may decide that you have a spiritual gift which did not emerge as a result of the inventory process. You may also be surprised by a spiritual gift which emerged. If either of those is the case, visit about the results with someone who knows you well. You may decide that you do have a spiritual gift which needs further development. You may decide that something you had thought was a spiritual gift may not actually be so. And you may decide that the assessment process was simply wrong at a particular point. In the end, you want to trust your own reflection and prayer rather than this or any other assessment process.

Spiritual Gifts Assessment

Respond to each statement which follows using this numerical system:

5 = This is highly descriptive of me virtually all of the time.

4 = This is descriptive of me most of the time.

3 = This is descriptive of me some of the time.

2 = This is descriptive of me only rarely.

1 = This is not descriptive of me.

It is very important for you to respond to these statements in terms of how you actually are rather than in terms of how you feel you should be. Don't be shy about acknowledging strengths, and don't feel badly because some statements are not descriptive of you. There are no "right" or "wrong" answers – only honest descriptions.

> ***Don't spend too much time thinking about a particular item. Go with your first impression, or leave the item blank and return to it later.***

_____ 1. I am able to convey ideas and insights in a way that motivates people to want to learn more.

_____ 2. I speak the truth about what I feel is right even when that is unpopular and hard for other people to accept.

_____ 3. I am willing to accept responsibility for organizations or groups that lack a clear sense of direction or leadership.

_____ 4. In the midst of other activities, I find myself focusing on the needs of another person and praying for that individual.

_____ 5. I feel that an important purpose of my home is to be a place to care for others, including people who are not part of my family.

_____ 6. I find satisfaction in working behind the scenes to help others make the most of their gifts and abilities.

_____ 7. I find pleasure in sharing my material resources with persons in need.

_____ 8. I cultivate relationships with persons who do not know Christ so that I can lead them to Him.

_____ 9. I can empathize with people who are going through difficult times and find meaning in involving myself in their healing processes.

_____ 10. I enjoy developing my skills in communicating through music, drama, or other art forms.

_____ 11. I am fulfilled when I am able to build or create something that helps the church or other people.

_____ 12. I am able to recognize what people truly want to communicate both from what they say and from what they do not say.

_____ 13. I find pleasure in learning about how organizations function.

_____ 14. People say they learn a lot from my teaching, and they seem motivated to want to learn more on their own.

_____ 15. I am willing to accept personal suffering and criticism if it will result in myself and others growing closer to God or doing the right thing by God's standards.

_____ 16. I've given leadership to groups which have sensed God's presence or gained a sense of purpose even in the middle of difficult times.

_____ 17. A day does not seem complete to me unless I have spent time praying for the needs of other individuals, of the church, and of the world.

_____ 18. I enjoy doing all that I can to help new people feel that they belong.

____ 19. I like to encourage others by serving wherever and whenever there is a need.

____ 20. I find significant meaning in knowing my financial support makes a difference in the ministries of the church or of another service organization.

____ 21. After I lead people to a closer relationship with God, I guide them into deeper discipleship and service.

____ 22. I find meaning in motivating others to have more concern about the health of their souls.

____ 23. I can communicate my sense of God more through music or other artistic means than through conversation.

____ 24. I can fashion raw materials into finished objects.

____ 25. I can continue to maintain a positive relationship with people even when it's necessary to express substantial disagreement or to raise questions about what they're doing.

____ 26. I can grasp the overall purpose or goals of an organization or group and work out plans for accomplishing them.

____ 27. I can draw other people into considering how their relationships with God or a sense of meaning and purpose should affect their daily lives.

____ 28. Even in the face of criticism or pressure, I challenge people to examine their lives and change their direction when needed.

____ 29. I can decisively manage people and resources in positive ways to bring a vision or mission into reality.

____ 30. The names of people who are especially in need of God's help are never far from my mind.

____ 31. I enjoy providing food and lodging for people in need.

____ 32. I like to use my natural and my learned skills to enable the work of others.

_____ 33. When I know that someone else is in need of resources which I have, I don't worry about replenishing what I give.

_____ 34. When I tell others what God has done in my life, they respond with renewed faith of their own.

_____ 35. I can motivate others to their faith more seriously in their lives.

_____ 36. People accuse me of being temperamental like an artist.

_____ 37. I feel that I honor God with things I make by hand.

_____ 38. I can empathize with and help people who are resentful, angry, or confused.

_____ 39. I have skill in coordinating the gifts of people for greater effectiveness.

_____ 40. I love to help others gain greater skill in understanding and expressing themselves.

_____ 41. I can motivate others to use their faith in making decisions in both their private and their public lives.

_____ 42. I usually have a clear sense of what needs to be done in an organization and can motivate others in that direction.

_____ 43. People frequently express appreciation to me for my having continued to remember them in my prayers.

_____ 44. I readily reach out to persons needing physical or emotional encouragement.

_____ 45. When I see a wide range of needs, I want to help with as many as I can.

_____ 46. I have been successful at earning or discovering significant amounts of money for the Lord's work.

_____ 47. I want people around me to know I am a Christian and hope that may provide opportunities to help them draw closer to Christ.

_____ 48. I am able to strengthen people who are wavering in their sense of purpose in life.

_____ 49. Through my artistic expressions, people have gained deeper insights into themselves or into the spiritual life.

_____ 50. I can design and build things to help the church or other organizations better serve people.

_____ 51. I show my concern by helping people find practical solutions to spiritual, relational, or personal struggles.

_____ 52. I like to improve the efficiency of organizations with which I work.

_____ 53. I enjoy finding practical guidance in the Bible and sharing that help with others.

_____ 54. I feel compelled to confront people when they display behaviors or attitudes which are destructive.

_____ 55. I can enthusiastically organize people to achieve goals which I feel are important.

_____ 56. I have had times when I was so absorbed in my prayers for the needs of others that I lost all track of time.

_____ 57. I like to help new people get acquainted with others in the church and in other settings.

_____ 58. I believe there is spiritual significance in the routine tasks I do for others.

_____ 59. Because I want to see significant things happen in ministry, I give more than a tithe (over 10%).

_____ 60. I continually seek to find different or better ways to share my faith with others.

_____ 61. I enjoy reaching out to people in settings like hospitals, nursing homes, or prisons.

_____ 62. I like the challenge of communicating with variety and creativity.

_____ 63. I can visualize how something should be constructed before I build it.

_____ 64. People tell me that my patient and understanding listening helps them clarify their thoughts.

_____ 65. Once I know what the goal is, I have skill at developing the strategy to meet it.

_____ 66. I always find myself learning more as I have opportunity to teach others.

_____ 67. I have had times when a concern was so heavy on my heart that I had to speak out no matter what the price.

_____ 68. Others seek me out to give leadership to various causes or organizations.

_____ 69. When I am deep into prayer for others, I often find myself communicating in images or feelings more than in words.

_____ 70. I feel that entertaining others in my home, at the church, or in other settings is one of the best ways that I am personally able to nurture genuine community.

_____ 71. I enjoy doing a variety of odd jobs around the church or other organizations to help meet the needs of people.

_____ 72. I am able to motivate others to financially support worthy causes.

_____ 73. I have the patience to work with another person over a long period of time in order to eventually bring that individual to faith in Christ.

_____ 74. I find great meaning in reaching out to persons at their times of greatest need no matter what the problem.

_____ 75. I enjoy developing my skills in the arts through music, crafts, drama, or other media.

_____ 76. I am gifted at putting things together and making them work.

_____ 77. I can generally help people see their problems from a new perspective and work toward a solution that is right for them.

_____ 78. I am good at and find pleasure in organizing many kinds of projects.

_____ 79. On the whole, I would rather teach a class or group than simply be a spectator.

_____ 80. I can confront people with problems in their own lives, in the church, or in society in a way that causes them to rethink their positions rather than simply be angry.

_____ 81. I can lead others through the development of a vision for their work together.

_____ 82. Praying for others several times a day feels almost as natural to me as breathing.

_____ 83. I feel a true calling to help new people become fully integrated into the life of the church or other organizations.

_____ 84. While I am often not the one giving direct leadership, a great many things in the organizations to which I belong would not get done without my willingness to do what is needed.

_____ 85. I give generously to God's work and genuinely do not seek or want any recognition or reward for what I do.

_____ 86. I feel that God often brings me into contact with people who need to discover or to rediscover Christ.

_____ 87. When people are going through difficult times, I am able to encourage them to maintain their faith and to do all they can to respond positively to the problems they face.

_____ 88. I feel that I have been especially gifted in terms of music, drama, painting, or another art form.

_____ 89. I have the ability to build or make things which will facilitate the work of the church or of other service organizations.

_____ 90. I am able to help people face the truth about themselves and their relationships with others when necessary to help them work through their problems.

_____ 91. I am generally known as an efficient person who keeps track of things and follows through well.

When you've completed all 91 assessment items, transfer your scores to the chart which appears on pages 46 and 47. Add each line across, producing a total on the right-hand side of page 47. Then transfer your highest scores to the chart below. Add your own comments about each spiritual gift which is listed. Are there any surprises? Are the results what you expected? Are you pleased with the results? Disappointed with the results?

Four Gifts with Highest Scores	Comments

If you invited one or more others to complete the assessment for you, compare their scores with your own. If there are significant discrepancies, talk about those with the person or persons who completed the assessment for you. Be open to what they have to say, but ultimately have confidence in your own perceptions.

Some Common Observations
About the Spiritual Gifts Assessment

1. **I only have one or two clear spiritual gifts by this system. My other scores are all much lower.** Don't be concerned. Some persons only have one or two spiritual gifts as measured by this kind of system. What's important is thinking about the gifts that you have and developing them as effectively as possible. (Occasionally a person will be uncomfortable responding to items in positive ways and will end up with scores that are artificially low. You may want to try completing the assessment again, this time thinking more positively about yourself!)

2. **I really have seven or eight spiritual gifts that all have very high scores.** Then you are probably blessed with an above average number of spiritual gifts. This isn't a matter for pride since gifts come to us from God rather than from our own effort, but it does mean that you may have many opportunities to be of help to others.

3. **I know that I have skills and abilities in an area in which I had a very low score on the assessment.** Remember that spiritual gifts are not the same as skills and abilities. You may be doing excellent work in an area that isn't really one of spiritual giftedness for you. On the other hand, it's also possible that the problem is with the assessment instrument itself. This is not a perfect system! Think about it, pray about it, and visit with others about it.

4. **I am almost shocked by how high my score was on one or two of the items. I really didn't think of myself as being gifted in those areas.** It's always possible that the assessment process is at fault; but generally you should take very seriously any new areas of giftedness which emerge from this process. You may find that you'll have wonderful opportunities to develop the gift or gifts and that new directions will open for you.

Teaching	1-	14-	27-	40-
Prophecy	2-	15-	28-	41-
Leadership	3-	16-	29-	42-
Intercession	4-	17-	30-	43-
Hospitality	5-	18-	31-	44-
Helps/Service	6-	19-	32-	45-
Generosity	7-	20-	33-	46-
Evangelism	8-	21-	34-	47-
Encouragement	9-	22-	35-	48-
Artistic Expression	10-	23-	36-	49-
Craftsmanship	11-	24-	37-	50-
Counseling	12-	25-	38-	51-
Administration	13-	26-	39-	52-

53-	66-	79-	Total-
54-	67-	80-	Total-
55-	68-	81-	Total--
56-	69-	82-	Total-
57-	70-	83-	Total-
58-	71-	84-	Total-
59-	72-	85-	Total-
60-	73-	86-	Total-
61-	74-	87-	Total-
62-	75-	88-	Total-
63-	76-	89-	Total-
64-	77-	90-	Total-
65-	78-	91-	Total-

All of us who call ourselves Christian have an obligation to live out our faith in the secular world as well as in the life of the church. Bivocational ministers, who often work at a secular job in addition to pastoring, have much to teach the rest of us about discipleship in all settings.

Chapter Three
Bivocational Ministry

The gifts he gave were that some would be apostles,
some prophets, some evangelists, some pastors
and teachers, to equip the saints for the work of
ministry, for building up the body of Christ, until
all of us come to the unity of the faith and of the
knowledge of the Son of God, to maturity, to the
measure of the full stature of Christ.

Ephesians 4:11-13

In 1997 the Brethren Academy for Ministerial Leadership and Christian Community began a cooperative study on bivocational ministry in the Church of the Brethren. General surveys were distributed through all the districts (the regional structure of the denomination) in the United States. Over 250 individuals responded, and 62 requested a more detailed follow-up survey specifically related to the personal experiences bivocational ministers have had in the church. The study was designed to understand the impact this type of ministry has on the lives of bivocational pastors, their families, and the members of their congregations.

The term "bivocational" implies that the minister has been trained or is skilled in a trade or an occupation in addition to the local church pastorate. Of course, a minister does not necessarily have to also work in a secular trade to be considered bivocational. Some may work in another paid ministry position (chaplain at a children's home, for example); and some are retired persons receiving pension income from other work they have done.

Sixty-seven percent of the general survey respondents indicated that they are or once were bivocational ministers. Only seven percent of the bivocational respondents stated that they had another professional ministry position in addition to their pastoral position. Roughly 33 percent described their additional employment as being connected with a business or farm they owned, while 60 percent worked as an employee or in a professional field. Examples of secular occupations and fields which we found in the survey:

social worker	plumber	doctor
principal	government work	banking
clerk	physician	journalism
teacher	electrician	sports coach
real estate	business owner	computer design

Training for Bivocational Ministry

Bivocational respondents were asked to indicate what level of education they had completed at what type of educational institution. Only 35% of the bivocational ministers surveyed had earned a seminary degree. Eleven percent of them listed Circleville, Bridgewater, and Temple as colleges which offered bivocational training. One-third of the bivocational respondents said that they had earned a graduate degree in their non-ministerial field. The average number of years spent training for ministry (4 years) was very similar to the average number of years spent training for the non-ministerial position (3.45 years). The ministerial training, however, was more likely to have been through undergraduate study or a denominational guided study program than through graduate-level seminary training.

Some bivocational ministers received their training and education for both occupations at about the same time. The majority, however, decided to become employed in a bivocational capacity after they had completed college or other training for secular employment. Sixty-six percent stated that their first employment was in a non-ministerial occupation; 26 percent were employed in the ministerial position first; and only 8% started both at the same time.

Whether or not a minister was employed in a secular position first does, in fact, have some impact on the reasons for being bivocational. Although financial need was cited as an important reason for having two vocations by both groups, those who chose a secular job after they were already in ministry were more likely to list need for greater income as an incentive than those who chose ministry after their secular occupation. By the same token, those who were in non-ministerial positions first were slightly more likely to state that calling was an important reason for joining the ministry.

In other words, the reasons for choosing to be bivocational differ between those who were originally ministers and those who followed the call later in life. This may affect their experience of bivocational ministry. Both groups, however, felt they had received a clear call to ministry. The following chart shares the reasons which those surveyed gave for choosing to be bivocational ministers.

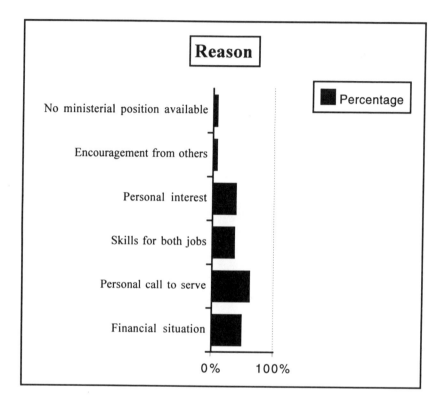

The category "no ministerial position available" was chosen by those who sought ministerial positions because of their calling or training but were unable to find such a position. They then found employment in a secular field.

The demands of two occupations can certainly be a source of pressure. The majority of the bivocational ministers surveyed stated that they were involved with ministry on a part-time (49%) or time-share (35%) basis. The time-share basis means that the ministerial responsibility is shared with one or more other persons (which often happens with the "free ministry" model). The majority of those working on a time-share basis were part-time. The following chart shows the amount of time spent in the ministerial part of bivocational work:

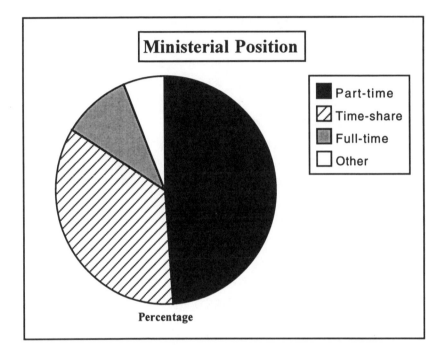

Some of those who checked the "other" category indicated that the time taken by the ministerial position is seasonal–there are months when they work full-time at it and months when they work considerably less.

Forty-eight percent of those who indicated that they were bivocational pastors work full-time in the non-ministerial position, and 32% indicated part-time work in that position. The others experienced a wider range of hours in the non-ministerial work, and a few were retired from their secular work though still see themselves as bivocational.

The average number of hours spent working as a minister among the bivocational clergy surveyed ranged from 20 to 30 hours a week; the average number of hours spent in the non-ministerial position ranged from 20 to 40 hours a week. It was not unusual to have bivocational ministers indicating that they work a total of more than sixty hours a week.

The Art of Bivocationalism

Being a bivocational minister is somewhat of an art, since it continually involves juggling priorities between two vocations. Our study clearly shows that some clergy are more comfortable than others with this balancing act, and we'll have more to say about this in the next chapter.

Time management is obviously an important skill for a bivocational minister. The success of bivocational clergy at managing both positions depends in good measure on the type of secular career chosen. Bivocational respondents overwhelmingly preferred being self-employed as the best option for a complementary vocation with ministry, simply due to the fact that self-employment is flexible enough to allow schedule changes with little notice. Careers that allow for emergency hospital calls, crisis counseling, and conducting funerals are almost a necessity for bivocational ministry, according to those completing the surveys. Those in a time-share (free ministry) position could handle less flexible secular work if another person on the team had greater flexibility. Those jobs labeled as "people occupations" (social work, education, banking, and health services) were viewed by bivocational ministers and by others completing the surveys as complementary to the kind of work that is done in the church.

Bivocational ministry calls for special training and self-exploration in addition to theology and caregiving skills. For those already employed who are answering the call to ministry, there are programs which offer training to individuals and to congregations without the commitment to full-time seminary study. In the Church of the Brethren, the main programs available are known as TRIM (Training in Ministry) and EFSM (Education for a Shared Ministry). Refer to chapter five for more details. Some of those completing our surveys felt that a seminary degree should be required even of a bivocational minister, and there are denominations which have little flexibility on that requirement.

Many of the respondents stated that communication, sociology/psychology, business administration, and management courses enhanced their preparation for ministry. Others asserted that a strong biblical background, solid theology, and knowledge of denominational history were very important in becoming an effective minister. The need to prepare oneself emotionally for bivocational ministry was also considered very important.

Congregational Support for Bivocational Ministry

Eighty-one percent of all respondents to our surveys were in favor of encouraging bivocational ministry. Reasons given for the encouragement ranged from "it is certainly a New Testament model and we are a New Testament Church" to "may be the only way small churches can have a pastor." Another respondent believed that:

**A
positive
view!**

> *It (bivocational ministry) could help alleviate
> our shortage of pastors. Carefully selected, a
> second vocation can broaden the pastor's outlook,
> get him/her more in touch with 'real life.' A second
> skill could contribute directly to his/her ministry.
> However, care needs to be taken so that there is
> no conflict in any way.*

Acting as an advisor to seminary students provides an avenue for introducing people to the concept of bivocational ministry. When asked whether they have advised seminary students to become bivocational, about half of the bivocational respondents (55%) said that they had. Some were uncertain about doing so, due to the difficult experiences as bivocational ministers that they had experienced.

One respondent acknowledged encouraging bivocational ministry but said: "I did so with a guarded heart. What is the church offering? What will you need? What can a part-time job provide? How much time should you give in contrast with what the church can pay?" There was tremendous concern among the bivocational respondents about how much the congregation is willing to support a bivocational minister, not only financially but also spiritually and emotionally. Those who practice the plural ministry (free ministry) model seem to have greater internal support from other team ministers as well as from the lay members. The following comment demonstrates this position:

**A team
approach
to
bivocational
ministry**

> *There are Godly leaders in congregations that
> enjoy their jobs and can help out greatly in the
> ministry. I do not encourage people to be
> bivocational by themselves. The plurality is so
> much better for the congregation and the
> ministers. We need in the pulpits people who are
> skilled in other areas. The people identify well*

| *with these pastors and are encouraged to do their part in the church.*

Another survey respondent declared that bivocational ministry is not something to be encouraged: "It benefits the church at the expense (financially and otherwise) of the pastor. There may be rare exceptions where it would be mutually beneficial." This remark reflects the strain felt by bivocational ministers and the necessity for support not only by their families, but also by friends, colleagues, and the congregation.

A majority of the bivocational ministers surveyed (61%) felt somewhat high to very high levels of stress in having two occupations. A smaller percentage (39%) did not experience high levels of stress. Those in the plural ministry (with a team approach to the bivocational work) were less likely to experience high stress than those who became bivocational out of economic necessity and/or those who are pastoring a congregation by themselves.

The chart which follows shows the support or influence of people by category on the decision to become a bivocational pastor, according to the perceptions of those pastors. The monetary support column refers to financial help with training for bivocational ministry.

Overwhelming praise and encouragement came from parents, friends, congregational members, and other ministers. Overall, members of one's church were most supportive with financial aid, praise, and initiating the idea or influencing the decision; discouragement of bivocational ministry by any source was minimal but was most likely to come from parents or teachers.

Source of Support	Monetary Support	Praise/ Encouragement	Influence Decision	Discourage Decision	Other Support
Parents	18%	75%	10%	13%	8%
Friends	5%	78%	18%	5%	10%
Teachers	0%	38%	5%	10%	15%
Church members	33%	80%	28%	8%	10%
Other Ministers	0%	78%	20%	5%	8%

While serving as a bivocational pastor, most survey respondents felt supportiveness from the congregation they served. Their perception of attitudes of church members toward them:

Level of Church Member Support	Percent of Bivocational Pastors Who Felt Support
Totally Supportive	59%
Somewhat Supportive	26%
Uneasy, But okay	4%
Express Discontent	11%
Highly Non-supportive	0%

The church members who express discontent tend to do so largely out of a desire to have a full-time pastor rather than out of lack of appreciation for the individual minister who is currently serving them.

The bivocational ministers who responded to our survey also indicated that they felt less supportiveness in their ministry from other clergy than they did from the members of the church they served. These references were not to other clergy who might be on a free ministry team with them but rather to their colleagues in neighboring congregations. Some felt that those who were full-time pastors with graduate seminary degrees looked down on people serving in part-time capacities without graduate degrees.

The bivocational minister continually works at balancing the various demands on his or her time. All of us can learn from the experiences of bivocational clergy

Chapter Four

Balancing Secular Work And Ministry

Therefore, since it is by God's mercy that we are engaged in this ministry, we do not lose heart.
2 Corinthians 4:1

The respondents to the bivocational survey made it clear that being an effective pastor means finding harmony between one's personal life and the demands of ministry. Learning to balance secular work and ministry is perhaps the most difficult task for a bivocational minister, and that has to be accomplished without destroying the quality of home life in the process. Each minister uses a slightly different approach to juggling the schedules and making the most out of both vocations.

Overwhelmingly, respondents stated lack of time was the number one problem as a bivocational minister:

- Not enough time for preparing sermons.
- Not enough time to give attention to the pastoral needs of the congregation.
- Not enough time for self-fulfilling activities.
- Not enough time to spend with one's family.

The issue of the family suffering as a result of the demands of two vocations comes out strongly through the comments of the respondents, including this observation:

Like many others, this bivocational pastor felt that the family often suffers.

You are always very busy. You never seem to have quite enough time to do everything you would like to do. Your family will be the first to suffer if you allow yourself to be spread too thin. This I perceive to be the greatest negative aspect of bivocational ministry. You tend not to take time just for yourself or your family and those relationships suffer.

Some believed that they lacked time to prepare adequately for the Sunday sermon, since it is often difficult to "change gears" from working in the non-ministerial position. Others felt that being available 24 hours-a-day to serve the needs of the members, especially in emergency situations, was a challenge. Meetings, funerals, and classes were presented as obstacles in managing one's time. A few mentioned that it was difficult to fulfill expectations that church members had of the bivocational minister. For example, one pastor wrote:

> *Perceived as making too much money. Congregational jealously ("We want you all the time."). Constant tug of war for your time. Expected to do a full-time job as a part-time minister.*

A constant theme in the survey responses was a conviction that the bivocational pastor is under greater pressure than a full-time pastor to be well-organized and to develop good time management skills. One bivocational pastor observed that this can cause friction with other pastors: "The biggest negative has been other ministers. It is probably a function of my daily profession, but I like to be organized and strategic in planning and making things happen. I have not found other ministers to be the best in planning and executing creatively." Others can become resentful of someone who places more priority on organization. Tension with other clergy can be especially awkward if they are part of the same ministry team for a congregation.

Stresses and Strains

Several bivocational ministers expressed the concept that they were serving "two masters." That can affect the minister emotionally, mentally, physically, and even spiritually. One pastor observed that the downside of having two jobs is revealed in "preoccupation with the task rather than the leadership." Another felt that being able to excel in either area was out of the question. Risks included not only low pay for work that wasn't satisfactory but having all other aspects of one's life become fractured as well. Being accessible to members and to denominational staff may be slighted in the process of trying to keep up with the daily demands of two jobs. Faced with too many pressures from too many different directions, a bivocational minister runs the risk of becoming alienated from his or her own congregation. The following comment reveals significant stress from bivocational ministry:

> *Bivocational churches usually have low self-esteem, which means low giving and too high expectations which equals stress. You feel out of the loop with other pastors and have very limited support. It is also difficult to just take off your work hat and put*

on your robe. You feel like two different people.

Many bivocational ministers felt that they needed more emotional preparation to deal with all the issues coming at them from many sides. Yet most affirmed that in spite of many pressures, they "did not lose heart" (2 Corinthians 4:1). The bivocational ministers who responded to our survey, for the most part, believed that the negative aspects of handling two jobs were of minimal significance in comparison to the positive experiences that came out of their work as bivocational ministers.

Looking at the Bright Side of Bivocational Ministry

The respondents to our survey listed a wide variety of benefits from being a bivocational minister. For example:

- Many, especially those serving very small congregations, felt that extra income was a valuable reward for having two jobs. While they worked more hours than with a single job, they also enjoyed greater financial security.

- A few liked the fact that they were not totally dependent on the congregation for their income. These respondents felt that not having to worry about the financial benefits was an important component in fulfilling their call to do God's will. Most in the plural or free ministry accepted only expense reimbursement from the church.

- Many liked the fact that church work was quite different from secular work. The diversity made it easier to maintain perspective, and they enjoyed the greater variety of activities.

- Being able to see solid results from one's secular work provided greater satisfaction when pastoral work could not show as immediate a result for the effort expended. Getting into a vocation apart from the church allowed a more apparent sense of freedom and well-being; and therefore, less feeling of dependence on "things going well at the church."

- Several felt that the church was strengthened because people knew that the part-time bivocational pastor couldn't do everything. Thus there was a greater willingness of church members to assume major leadership roles.

- Several also pointed out that involvement in the community through secular work opened many doors for ministry. It provided the opportunity to truly be Christ's presence to others in the world.

Perhaps the greatest reward to come out of the bivocational experience, however, is that many became more connected with their own members. This was the most common response shared among almost all who responded to the survey. One respondent shared this sentiment:

> *You have more in common with your congregation. You work in a vocation just as most of them do, so you can better understand the pressures and concerns they are dealing with from day to day. The fact that you are sacrificing in your life to be in ministry to them gives you*

the right to speak to them of sacrificial living. The fact that you are willing to give up something in life to serve the church encourages others to serve and this becomes contagious.

When another vocation provides an opportunity to identify with congregational members in their everyday pressures and struggles, witnessing and counseling to others takes on a whole new meaning. Members may be more willing to support a minister who is bivocational because that pastor can relate on their level, rather than being isolated in an "ivory tower."

Many believed that being a "minister of the people" resulted in greater depth, especially in the secular workplace. Reaching out to fellow employees and those in the wider community expanded a minister's perspective on the realm of spirituality. They felt that they were actually doing the type of witnessing that Jesus had taught his followers to do. Linking the secular and the sacred heightens a bivocational minister's sense of personal spirituality in relation to others. Understanding how personal struggles are dealt with by people at their places of work inspires a minister to connect the theology of the Church and the teachings of Scripture to action in the real world. Many felt they were better able to write sermons that members could connect with and apply to their lives because of the bivocational nature of their ministry.

There are other ways in which secular work enhances ministry and ministry brings fulfillment to secular work. Greater sensitivity and compassion are certainly benefits, particularly when counseling individual members or families of the church. This allows church members to view the minister as "one of them." This link also serves to encourage active participation in church affairs and worship by laity. Bivocational ministers find that members are more willing to help out with various tasks, including administration, building maintenance, and worship. The respondents felt that when every member accepts responsibility for the growth of the church, a healthy and vital church is the result.

Skills that a bivocational minister brings from the secular work environment can enhance his or her effectiveness in dealing with some of the work of the church. These include organization/administrative skills, time management strategies, and conflict resolution. Many find that what they learn in the non-ministerial vocation is highly compatible with what they need to accomplish as a minister.

Likewise, a bivocational minister can apply experience in the church to the secular realm. This is especially true when meeting new people in order to build a bridge between church and community. Not only is witnessing to others and welcoming them to their local congregation an important aspect of this, but also making a difference in the quality of community life. A powerful example of this is revealed in one minister's efforts at reaching out to others:

A strong example of service resulting from bivocational work

I served in the free ministry. . . for more than twenty-one years and I was employed by a wholesale food distributor. When the thought of retirement came, it was really scary because I didn't know what I could do with myself! Through working with the food industry I know I appreciated meeting people, so I started a food

**Help to over
200 places!**

outreach ministry by giving 40 lb. boxes of apples to needy places. In four years this little outreach ministry has grown to over two hundred places, from Harrisburg to Philadelphia– homeless shelters, homes for AIDS victims, drug & alcohol rehab, shelter for abused women and children, etc. I don't tell you this to "blow my own horn" but I believe that my "other work experience" has helped my "church ministry" and the ministry of helping the least of my brothers and sisters.

The Need for Congregational and Denominational Support

Bivocational ministers still need tremendous encouragement and support not only from family, friends, and church members, but also from within the denominational structure and from each other. Support groups for bivocational ministers could be helpful in some settings. Ministerial meetings, conferences, seminars, and workshops are also opportunities to connect to others like themselves, when those meetings are held at times they can participate.

Local plural or free ministry churches, served by a team of part-time clergy, already have an internal support system. But many bivocational clergy are alone, and a few are even serving in more than one church on top of trying to balance a secular occupation. On-line chat rooms and web-pages may serve to link ministers to one another in order to discuss the issues surrounding their calling. Publishing a newsletter or bulletin strictly for bivocational ministers might be helpful in some denominations or even across denominational lines. It would at least be helpful if those responsible for denominational publications would select content and edit with an awareness that some clergy are bivocational. Sessions for bivocational ministers held at the time of annual denominational meetings could also provide opportunity for mutual support and exchange of helpful strategies.

But perhaps the greatest support for bivocational ministers comes from people within their own congregation. Involving laity in doing more in the church would not only lift the burden of responsibility from the minister's shoulders but also give reassurance that the congregation has confidence in the growth of the church. Lay members have many opportunities to be involved in the church in ways that enhance pastoral ministry:

visitation	caregiving	teaching
administration	committee work	newsletters
music	preaching/worship	counseling
maintenance	stewardship	youth work
evangelism	help to the hungry	missions

Many respondents noted the tremendous need for the gifts of all the members of the church to be utilized. One expressed it this way:

We have lost our art of doing this (calling members to ministry). We need to stress on naming and discerning gifts of the spirit in our members.

Some pointed out that clergy trying to do too much on behalf of the congregation may keep members from developing their own spiritual gifts. One survey respondent said:

*Members could be alive and creative if pastors learned
to share and refer. Healthy churches are churches where
ownership is claimed by members.*

Finally, this response is particularly poignant:

*We need to emphasize the "priesthood of all believers."
We all have a ministry. Clergy need to be about the task
of setting people free for ministry after they help them
define and discover their spiritual gifts. My pastoral
vision is: to equip, empower, and set people free in the
ministry of Jesus.*

When bivocational ministry results in members of the
congregation accepting greater responsibility to utilize their own
spiritual gifts, a church has the potential not only to survive but
to flourish.

Bivocational clergy work at balancing secular work with the
practice of ministry. All of us who call ourselves Christian,
however, have an obligation to be Christ's presence in our places
of work, our neighborhoods, and our homes. That doesn't mean
that we inappropriately witness or attempt to proselytize
persons of other faith traditions in the work setting, but it does
mean we take seriously the reality that we are Christ's presence
to a world in need. That should affect how we treat other people,
how we make decisions, and how we manage our time. It means
being open to opportunities to naturally and appropriately share
our faith with others and invite those who do not have a church
home to become part of our congregations.

Perhaps there is a sense in which we are all called to

bivocational ministry–in that we are to use our spiritual gifts not only in the life of the church but in the world in which we live. The next chapter explores the role that training plays in equipping us for meaningful ministry.

Training can come in many different ways including formal classroom instruction, the Internet, reading, and mentoring both by phone and in person.

Chapter Five

The Need for Trained Ministers

Go therefore and make disciples of all nations,
baptizing them in the name of the Father and of
the Son and of the Holy Spirit, and teaching them
everything that I have commanded you. And
remember, I am with you always, to the end of
the age.

Matthew 28:19-20

Beginning with Pentecost, the Church has had a history of calling out and training leadership. Before his ascension, Jesus commissioned his followers *to go and make disciples*, including the key phrase *teaching them all I have taught you* (Matthew 28:20). With those words, leadership training became a priority for disciples of Jesus, past and present.

Acts 2 describes the coming of the Holy Spirit which marked the beginning of the church and the first leadership crisis. Following the events of Pentecost, the church began growing so rapidly that soon competent leadership was in short supply. Partially due to the shortage of trained leaders, the early church had to struggle to keep the story of Jesus and his teachings accurate. With the passing of time, it was inevitable that pieces of cultural and other religious traditions were woven into the fabric of this new "church." Without the constant reminders and teaching of the apostles, it would have been impossible to maintain the integrity of what Jesus had taught and modeled. Leadership training continued through preaching, through letters written to the churches, through mentoring new converts, through teaching small groups, and through the witness of lives given to Christ and the church at great sacrifice.

Clearly Jesus set the standard for calling and training leaders during his years on earth, and he gave his followers the Great Commission to continue doing the same. Throughout those early decades, the disciples effectively spread the Gospel message by modeling a training method Jesus had used. They moved from city to city teaching and training people who then became equipped to teach others. The church of today continues to use the traditional teaching techniques of the early apostles as well as new educational ideas. Training competent leaders was, and is, the key to continuing the Great Commission of Jesus. As we consider the incredible variety of cultural and political forces that the church encountered in the first two centuries, we better understand and appreciate the priority that early church leaders placed on accurate communication of the life and teachings of Jesus. To understand the ways in which outside forces can impact the church, a closer look at the last four decades of our own time can teach us a great deal.

What Happened?

In 1961, most Protestant and Anabaptist denominations were enjoying a time of steady growth. That was certainly true for the

Church of the Brethren (the denomination in which the bivocational study was conducted). Preparations were being made for continued growth with construction projects and new organizational plans in congregations and denominational agencies. But by the close of the decade, a shift had occurred and growth stopped. The next two decades were confusing and threatening, and the nineties found many local churches and entire denominations weaker numerically than in the early sixties.

Today much of the leadership in the church can well remember the time when churches were full, and they desperately want to reclaim the growth trend of the past. The "Protestant work ethic" took hold, and many dedicated Christians assumed that they were just not working hard enough. Many doubled their efforts without changing the overall trend. To some extent, everyone was caught in radical cultural changes that impacted American families and the churches they attended.

During the latter part of the twentieth century, the cultural expectations in the United States moved more and more toward professional specialists. For example, we expect that our medical care comes from a group of doctors, one of whom will know everything about a particular ailment (hopefully the one we have). Farmers have become specialists, or they use specialists whose expertise will fill in the gaps. Most of our commercial and institutional life is dependent upon persons who know a great deal about a special field.

This expectation has also influenced churches. The description of a well-trained pastor has changed during the past 50 years. A college educated and seminary trained pastor is the hoped-for standard for nearly all churches in most denominations. It is common for large congregations to search for a senior pastor with a doctoral degree, and large church staffs recognize specializations in youth work, Christian education, church music, and business administration.

> *However, this level of training for pastoral leadership has become problematic for many small congregations. A college and seminary education can easily cost the student $100,000 to $150,000. A congregation with a salary package of $20,000 cannot support a pastor with normal living expenses and a college debt to repay.*

Within the decades of the sixties, seventies, and eighties, the church in the United States and Canada felt the impact of a great cultural shift. Transportation systems were created to move large numbers of people across North America, to and through major cities. These cities became "hubs" for auto, truck, airline, and rail traffic. Due to migration of the younger generations to these hubs, urban population increased and rural population decreased.

Railroads and interstate highways passed through rural areas, but by design, also left them isolated. Small town public schools consolidated, and corporations bought up family farms. All of these factors had a major impact on small towns all across America. When a community lost the identity of its own school system, it didn't seem long before commerce and other services also left. As people followed bigger schools, bigger hospitals, and bigger shopping centers, they soon wanted bigger churches.

But churches were not as easily transported. As churches in rural areas experienced the population shift, which left them with fewer people, the response was to avoid moving by trying numerous church growth strategies in order to recreate the critical mass needed to continue the church in that place in the same way.

Most of those strategies were less than successful. The overwhelming desire to maintain or "save" the church has too often been motivated by "avoidance of change." To suggest that some changes should occur so other change does not have to occur is a "catch 22." For some people, "change" is the enemy, and it does not matter which change is suggested.

Rural communities are not alone in adjusting to cultural changes. Urban communities and their congregations also experienced population shifts as suburban communities were developed. Many large downtown congregations have lost membership and have discovered the necessity of change.

The truth is, however, that the rush of our culture toward "bigger" isn't always accompanied by "better." Many small congregations, rural or urban, are very healthy places to grow in faith and understanding of the Gospel of Jesus Christ. It is also true that in most of these healthy small congregations, *change is not the enemy.* They have learned how to stay focused on the foundational principles of their faith and meet people where they are in life's circumstances. That often means changes in worship style, music, time of services, and other areas which do not detract from sharing the love of Jesus with a hurting world. Small, healthy congregations are not intimidated by the fear of change. *But staying focused on the foundational elements of faith in the midst of change requires strong, well-trained leaders.*

Leadership Needs in Small Churches

A recent Church of the Brethren study reveals that of 1,180 persons serving in pastoral roles, more than half, 628, are part-time. Many of those pastors are by necessity bivocational. While that seems a rather high percentage of part-time clergy, most Protestant denominations have large numbers of churches which cannot support a full-time pastor. Those churches must be served by part-time pastors, or they must be yoked together into two-point, three-point, or even four-point charges in order to be staffed with full-time clergy. Here's how ministerial staffing looks in the Church of the Brethren:

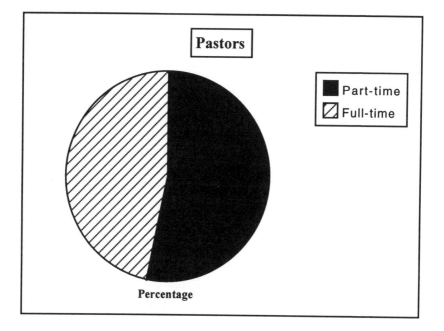

Sixty percent of the membership of the Church of the Brethren is located in 28% of the congregations, with the remaining 40% of the membership being distributed among the remaining 72% of the congregations, which all have fewer than 150 members. The significance of a membership of 150 is that often this is the critical number needed to support a full-time pastor. There are obviously some congregations whose financial resources allow them to adequately support a full time pastoral program with fewer than 150 members, and there are churches larger than that size which cannot afford a full-time pastor. There are also many pastors with a "full-time" title who serve with part-time salary. (In fact, the 1997 statistics for the Church of the Brethren indicate that there are 44 congregations with 50 or fewer members reported as having a full time pastoral program.)

The following chart is specific to the Church of the Brethren, but many larger denominations also have a large percentage of their churches which are relatively small.

1997 Statistics From the 1998
Church of the Brethren Year Book

Church Size	Number of Churches	Number of Members	% of Churches	% of Members
300+	105	47,348	10%	33%
200-299	112	26,128	10%	18%
100-199	292	40,905	27%	28%
1- 99	584	30,553	53%	21%

In his insightful book *The Small Membership Church* (Abingdon, 1994), Lyle Schaller compares denominations on the basis of the sixty-seventh percentile for average worship attendance. That means that two-thirds of the congregations in the denomination average less than that number in average worship attendance and that one-third average that number or more. Here are the sixty-seventh percentiles for some of the major denominations:

Denomination	2/3 of Congregations with Average Worship Attend. Below this Number
• Episcopal Church	165
• Evangelical Lutheran Church	157
• Presbyterian Church (U.S.A.)	124
• United Church of Christ	120
• American Baptist Churches	116
• Southern Baptist Convention	110
• Disciples of Christ	110
• Church of the Brethren	93
• United Methodist Church	87
• Free Methodist Church	73

When one considers that two-thirds of the churches in each denomination listed above are smaller than the average worship attendance given, it's clear that leadership for smaller congregations is an important issue.

The Silent Majority?

Even though *most of the persons* worshiping in a Church of the Brethren congregation on Sunday morning are being pastored by a minister with a full-time assignment, that does not mean that *most congregations* employ full-time pastors. In fact, as already shared, more than half of the churches in this denomination have part-time, often bivocational, pastors. Some denominations which are organized with more two-point, three-point, and even four-point pastoral charges in order to utilize full-time pastors still have a majority of the congregations which are relatively small. There are many respects in which small congregations are the majority—in some ways a "silent majority."

Maintaining the organizational structure of a small congregation often results in volunteers filling niches within the system with little or no formal training. Informal training often means "on-the-job-training" (OJT) and is used to prepare persons for their roles. OJT can be effective but not if it results in a "sink-or-swim" situation. To avoid burnout and frustrated leaders, training must be offered which is relevant to the task and the context of the ministry.

In small congregations, not only are lay persons often caught without adequate training or preparation, but clergy leaders may also be called out with a limited amount of training. Bivocational ministers often find it difficult to earn a living, gain the necessary training, and also pastor a church.

Within the eighties and nineties, a cycle of fewer people from smaller congregations participating in leadership training and less awareness of their needs have helped to increase this "silent majority" of congregations whose voice is not heard and whose needs are not met. Training events increasingly are aimed at the needs of larger congregations and their pastors.

Bivocational pastors are not on the receiving end of many of the professional resources generally afforded to clergy. Professional growth events, conferences, and seminars are generally designed with schedules to accommodate full-time pastors. Thus a majority of the churches and their pastors in the Church of the Brethren are not able to fully participate in professional development models designed for larger congregations.

According to recent statistics in the Church of the Brethren, nearly 300 congregations were without permanent pastoral leadership for at least part of 1998. Most of them were "open" for worship on Sunday mornings with the assistance of a speaker or preacher from somewhere nearby. Congregations whose norm is "pulpit supply" for worship can soon lose their identity and sense of vision for mission. Even though there is a ready supply of recommended speakers and guest preachers, each will likely have a passion for a particular mission or local ministry (perhaps their own), which eventually diffuses the vision of the congregation's mission. With someone new in the pulpit nearly every Sunday, regular attendance of the members often becomes inconsistent.

Ironically, sometimes there is more initiative within a congregation for inviting others to come and hear a special speaker than a permanent pastor. That too can be an unhealthy pattern, especially for small congregations. They actually experience "church-hoppers" (visitors who have no intention of becoming part of the life of the church) looking for excitement in something new. It is very difficult for congregational leaders to plan ahead and be adequately prepared when attendance is inconsistent. It is also true that denominations can not plan well and be adequately prepared when congregations become "mission-hoppers" as they respond to all the opportunities presented by visiting ministers.

Within the context of these changes, denominational leaders

have had to get reacquainted with their constituency. It is easy to forget that so many of our congregations are small when the primary contact with them is in large group settings, such as regional judicatory and national meetings. Most of us want to maintain images of a larger church as the norm. Even congregations, now a fraction of their nineteen-sixties size, want to continue to operate like a larger church. Since denominations have placed so much emphasis on church growth programs over the last three decades, it is easy to mistake smallness for failure and something that must be corrected.

Many factors have contributed to the neglect and the problems of smaller congregations. As already shared, part of the difficulty originates in the congregations themselves resisting change. The cultural influence of a "bigger is better" mentality and the desire of people for greater specialization have also had impact. Another subtle but important factor is the reality that over the last three decades most seminaries have trained pastors with styles, skills, and expectations to serve larger congregations.

Within the Church of the Brethren, those trends are shifting. The General Board, the denomination's national headquarters, has been restructured to better respond to the needs of congregations of all sizes. Bethany Theological Seminary led the way for the denomination with a new approach to "congregationally-based education." The Brethren Academy for Ministerial Leadership, located at Bethany Seminary, has a mission for reaching small congregations with a variety of unique leadership development programs. Education For A Shared Ministry (EFSM) and Training In Ministry (TRIM) are two certificate programs offered through the Brethren Academy which are described in more detail later in this chapter.

We cannot afford to ignore the need to call and train new leaders, especially for small congregations. In addition to a pastoral shortage, laity have not been prepared adequately to step into leadership roles. Well-trained clergy and congregational members are needed to provide strength and continuity.

A warning to readers outside the Church of the Brethren!

The next section of this chapter is focused on training options within the Church of the Brethren. If you are a member of another denomination, you may want to skip this section. On the other hand, with bivocational pastors representing a valuable asset in many denominations, you may find these models of interest. And while these models are especially helpful in providing training to persons pastoring small membership congregations, the same models can help train bivocational pastors who are going to work part-time on the staff of a large congregation.

Training for Small Church Ministry

We are faced with the same dilemma today that threatened the early church 2000 years ago. Religious teachings can be easily twisted or manipulated to falsely confirm an individual's ideas and may miss the primary message of the Gospel of Jesus Christ. The risk to the Church is that unscrupulous writers, preachers, and teachers will become so powerfully attractive that well-meaning, but unknowing persons, will not seek further for truth. They are simply grateful to be made to feel secure by the "words and sounds" of their preacher/teacher. The pages of the New Testament tell of these same circumstances within the early church.

Any size church can be vulnerable to false teaching from self-proclaimed preachers with no accountability to a denomination.

In different circumstances, but for similar reasons as those faced by the early church, churches today are also attracted to individuals who proclaim a convenient or perhaps bizarre interpretation of what the message of the church should be. Without trained leaders, the Gospel can become unrecognizable in two or three generations.

The Brethren Academy for Ministerial Leadership is a vehicle for reaching small congregations with quality leadership training opportunities. The primary ministry training program, especially suited for bivocational ministers, is **Education for a Shared Ministry (EFSM)**. This program is co-sponsored by Bethany Theological Seminary (Richmond, Indiana), the Ministry Office of the Church of the Brethren (Elgin, Illinois), and participating districts and congregations. EFSM is directed through the Brethren Academy for Ministerial Leadership with offices at Bethany Seminary.

The genius of this program is that a minister-in-training is selected from within a congregation, along with five individuals for laity-in-training. Together they progress through a three year educational process with opportunity for the minister to be credentialed within the Church of the Brethren and for five lay persons to be trained for supporting roles within the ministry of that congregation. The program is especially designed to accommodate persons who are employed in secular work along with a vocation of ministry.

The educational components of EFSM are focused on the basic skills and knowledge of pastoral ministry. *Within the local church setting, students work on the following*:

1. **Ministerial skills:**
   Administration, Counseling, Preaching and Worship,
   and Teaching.

2. **Bible and Theology:**
   Old Testament Survey, New Testament Survey,
   Basic Beliefs, and Church History.

3. **Bethany Seminary Weekend:**
   A workshop in the congregation led by a
   teacher/student team from Bethany Seminary.

Outside the local setting, EFSM students will work on the
following:

1. **Orientation Week at Bethany Seminary which**
   provides an introduction to the program.

2. **Bethany Extension School or an equivalent event**
   which provides more academic content.

3. **The Church's Life and Mission, including attendance**
   at Annual Conference (the national meeting of the
   denomination), District Conference, a congregational
   goal setting process, and at least one ecumenical
   gathering.

Education for a Shared Ministry is especially helpful to small
congregations where the minister is, or would like to be,
bivocational and is unable to take a leave of absence for formal
training. The timeline for training is three years, beginning with
an orientation at Bethany Seminary. The curriculum (see the

outline on page 86) has flexibility to meet the needs of the persons involved, but prescribes the foundational training needed for ministry. A unique aspect of EFSM is the laity-in-training group that also experiences instruction. As a result of this program, a lasting model of leadership development is instilled within the congregation. The old cycle of "sink or swim" leadership training is broken! The EFSM model has been refined over a twenty-year period, and participating congregations have had good experiences with this nontraditional approach to learning.

Training in Ministry (TRIM) is a program that can be well-suited to equipping pastors for either full-time or bivocational ministry. This program requires more formal classroom experience than EFSM. Launched in 1987, TRIM features a flexible training model that utilizes locally accessible educational opportunities provided by colleges and church agencies, as well as graduate courses at the Seminary and/or Academy-sponsored training events. Under the direction of a seminary-trained district coordinator, TRIM students pursue curricular units in general education, Bible and theology, and ministry and ministry skills, and participate in an ongoing Ministry Formation Group.

The purpose of TRIM is to give persons the opportunity for ministry training in an academic setting while also receiving credits for practical experiences. For most TRIM graduates, the flexible program makes the difference in being able to complete training for ministry. TRIM is a certificate program through the Academy, although students may also earn degrees from accredited institutions in their geographic areas.

Whatever the option for leadership training, the primary

purpose is to preserve and pass on the knowledge of the foundational teachings of Jesus Christ. The presence of trained leadership in our midst will help keep us focused and energized for ministry.

Next Steps

Obviously it has not been possible in this chapter to cover the full range of training available for clergy and committed lay persons. Many persons who anticipate full-time ministerial service will continue to pursue a college degree and then a seminary degree. Volunteer lay leadership will continue to receive helpful instruction in on-the-job training, through reading, and in workshops at the local church, regional, and national levels.

There are several options for persons considering bivocational ministry. Consulting with appropriate regional denominational staff is a good first step. There are some ministers who are currently serving full-time but would have interest in expanding their options for placement as a bivocational pastor. It is important for these persons to assess their skills and talents which have potential for transfer to secular work. That information can be helpful in choosing a second career. Professional career counseling and completing a spiritual gifts inventory will also be beneficial (see chapters two and six).

Another possibility is that persons who are currently working in secular fields may want to assess their gifts and skills for ministry. Again, a spiritual gifts inventory and counsel with regional staff can be very helpful. In the Church of the Brethren, districts are responsible for reviewing applications and interviewing persons interested in ministry. Many people have found bivocational ministry very satisfying and exactly what the congregation needed. (See chapter three, chapter four, and the chart at the end of chapter six for more information on careers which are compatible with bivocational ministry.)

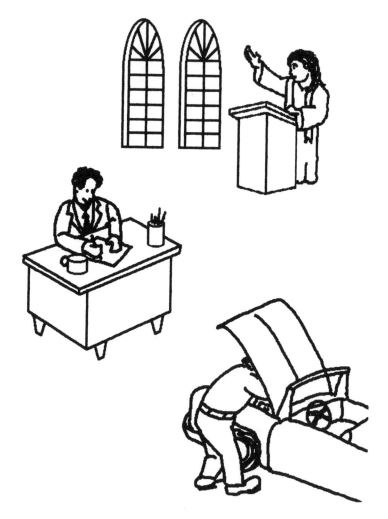

We all have a ministry in the church, in our places of work, in our homes, and in society as a whole. What is the particular ministry to which Christ is calling you?

Chapter Six
What Is Your Ministry?

I thank my God every time I remember you,
constantly praying with joy in every one of
my prayers for all of you, because of your
sharing in the gospel from the first day until
now.

Philippians 1:3-5

If you have not completed
the exercise to assess your
spiritual gifts which is in
the second chapter, you
should do so at this time.

What Is Your Ministry?

Paul thanked the Philippians for their involvement in sharing
the gospel. While Paul played a major role in the development of
the early church, he had deep appreciation for the work which
others did and saw others as sharing in the ministry with him.
Paul's eloquent words, especially in First Corinthians 12,
describe the concept of the body of Christ of which we are all a
part.

The chapters thus far have encouraged you to think about the
nature of ministry, whether carried out by full-time clergy,
bivocational clergy, or lay members of the church. In this chapter

we are encouraging you to think very personally about your own ministry. What is it to which God is calling you?

The spiritual gifts assessment in the second chapter has hopefully enabled you to better understand your own gifts for ministry. Now consider some different ways in which God may be giving you opportunity to utilize those gifts:

- By supporting and encouraging professional clergy.
- By making the most of your spiritual gifts in your involvement in the life of the church.
- By developing a ministry of compassion and witness in your secular employment.
- By seeking opportunities to carry out ministry in the community.
- By considering the possibility that God could be calling you to a bivocational or full-time ministry, if that has not already happened.

Supporting and Encouraging Professional Clergy

Thursday night, Brian lingered after the church computer task force meeting to visit privately with the pastor. "Beth," he said, "you really seemed on edge tonight."

She smiled and then shook her head. "Guess I did about bite poor Ralph's head off for suggesting that we change the word processing program. I wasn't very gracious. It's just that I couldn't face the idea of learning a whole new software program with everything else I have to do."

"I think we were all in agreement with you–even Ralph–once you'd explained why you were so upset. It isn't like you to react that strongly to a difference in opinion."

"And I've been doing more of that the last few months. I'm not getting enough sleep and feel stressed most of the time."

"I couldn't keep the pace you do," Brian said. "I suppose it isn't my business since I'm not on the pastor parish committee, but it concerns me that you're working so many hours and have three children."

"And a husband I don't see much of. I know that I need to slow the pace, but I can't seem to do it."

"I know you're very committed to the church, and we're all very thankful for the big increase in attendance and activity since you became our pastor. But we care about you, and it isn't right for you to be working this hard. What about asking the pastor parish committee to help you set some new priorities and arrange more time off? This church has four hundred members. Some of us ought to be able to lift a little of the load for you. If that won't do it, maybe we need to be looking for additional staff."

"I probably needed for someone to say that to me. I love what I do, and I love the people of the church. I keep feeling like it's all God's work and that I ought to get it done. But I know God doesn't intend for me to work all the time and neglect my family."

On his spiritual gifts assessment, Brian scored especially high on the gift of encouragement. He was practicing that gift in reaching out to his pastor. His initiative did result in her talking to the pastor parish committee and then the church board with the result that others picked up some responsibilities for her. A year later the church added an associate pastor to the staff.

Most ministers have high commitment to the church and a very strong work ethic. Because part of their work involves responding to crises in the lives of others, they don't always have the kind of control over their schedules which some persons in secular employment do. If you scored especially high on the gift of encouragement, one of the persons you should consider encouraging occasionally is the pastor! While most churches have a pastor parish committee, personnel committee, or other group concerned about supporting and encouraging the pastor, that doesn't replace the church as a whole encouraging and building up the pastor.

In fact, you don't have to possess the gift of encouragement to make a positive difference in the life of your pastor and as a consequence in the life of your church. Consider:

- Ways in which you can share appreciation with your pastor for the work which he or she is doing. That may take the form of personal comments, an occasional phone call, or a hand-written note. In our technological culture, e-mail may be another way to share your appreciation with the pastor.

- Ways in which you can positively interpret your pastor's work in the community. Consider saying to a friend who is not connected with a church: "We had a great sermon on Sunday. I really wish you'd come sometime to hear our pastor and find out what our church is like."

- Ways in which you can be supportive of your pastor to those in the congregation who are inclined to be critical. For example: "I know the pastor wasn't as well-prepared as usual today, but he stayed up all night with the youth at the lock-in. I'm just glad that he wants to spend time with the youth."

- Ways in which you can help your pastor by sharing information directly with him or her rather than becoming a participant in gossip. For example: "Bob, it sure doesn't matter to me, but I thought you would want to know that Mrs. Matthews has been complaining to a few people about it being a long time since you came for a visit."

- Ways you can be sensitive to staff members in addition to the pastor. Church members often have a tendency to treat associate pastors, youth workers, business administrators, and other professional staff as though they weren't quite as important as the pastor. Be sure you are sharing positive feedback with everyone on the staff–including secretaries and custodians.

Making the Most of Your Spiritual Gifts in the Church

Joanne's service to the church had primarily been as a teacher and as a member of the education committee. When she and her husband had joined the church twenty-five years ago, the church had been almost desperate for more teachers for their rapidly expanding Sunday school program. Joanne had volunteered to teach kindergarten, and her husband had taught junior highs.

Year-after-year, Joanne continued to teach: kindergarten, third grade, junior high, and then back to kindergarten. She had also served on the education committee for a long time. She was really glad to serve the church in whatever way she could and always discovered that she learned a lot herself in the process of preparing to teach. It occasionally seemed to her, however, that she had been pigeon-holed as an education person and that no one even considered asking her to do anything else in the church.

When she completed a spiritual gifts assessment, she was intrigued to find that her score on teaching was not one of her three highest. Her highest scores were first on administration, second on leadership, and third on giving. Since she so thoroughly enjoyed her position as a financial executive in a large company, it made sense that she had gifts in the areas of administration and leadership. Perhaps because of her interest in financial matters, she had always taken their giving to the church very seriously; but she had not considered the possibility that she might actually have a spiritual gift in that area.

As Joanne took a new look at the volunteer opportunities in the church, she realized that the idea of working on the church's finance committee or the church board was very appealing. She supposed it would be a shock for her to go onto the finance committee since that group was so male-dominated in her church. Yet in view of her secular work experience and her interest in giving, it began to surprise her that she had not been invited to be serve on that committee and that she had not thought of volunteering herself.

Joanne talked with the church personnel committee, which had supervised the spiritual gifts assessment process, and decided to start serving on the finance committee and on the church board. She was ready for a break from education work. The result was that the church's next financial campaign, which was headed by Joanne, was the most successful in percentage increase in the congregation's history.

You may already be working in the areas of the church which match with your strongest spiritual gifts. The existence of the gifts often does cause us to be pulled in particular directions, to more readily accept some opportunities for service and to decline others. Many people, however, sincerely wanting to serve the church in its areas of need, find themselves giving their time in areas far removed from their strongest spiritual gifts. Sometimes that work can be satisfying, and not everyone in that situation will want to change. Nevertheless, one of the major benefits of identifying your spiritual gifts should be a reassessment of the ways in which you are involved in the church.

Many churches are moving to spiritual gift assessments as a way to help people find the most fulfilling places to be involved in the life of the church. This approach to volunteer personnel in the church starts with the gifts of people and then looks at the ministry opportunities in the church. In most congregations, there will be sufficient diversity of gifts for people to work in the areas in which they have the greatest strength.

If you find your volunteer work in the church feeling more like an obligation than a fulfilling ministry, you may need to reassess what you have been doing. Working in the area of one's spiritual gifts can be an empowering experience; and a whole church full of people developing their spiritual gifts can have tremendous energy.

As you think about your spiritual gifts, you may also identify needs in the church which aren't currently being met but which are of interest and concern to you. Matt completed a spiritual gifts assessment similar to the one in chapter two of this book and discovered that his strongest spiritual gifts were in the areas of evangelism and hospitality. His church, however, had been doing very little in the area of evangelism; and its membership had been declining for almost twenty years. Most people in the church felt there was little they could do about the decline, that the values of unchurched people were just not compatible with those of church members.

Matt, however, felt like he knew many good people outside the church, including people who talked about their faith in God but who had rejected the church as an institution. He started wondering what he could do to get those people more involved in the life of his local church. He persuaded his pastor and the church board to help him form a small task force on evangelism, and they started developing plans to attract and invite new people to the church.

The task force spent two years at work before many results were evident. The first few potential members they got to visit the church didn't keep coming because they didn't feel warmly received. Thus the task force had to educate the congregation about how to show biblical hospitality to new people.

**Biblical
Hospitality**

*Biblical hospitality refers to the overall efforts of individuals and the church to help strangers feel welcome in their midst and become part of the life of the church. The spiritual gift of hospitality, described in chapter two of this book, certainly includes the ability to help people feel accepted and warmly received; but the spiritual gift includes an especially deep concern for those on the edges of society because of loneliness and poverty. Biblical hospitality is something to which everyone in the church is called; hospitality as a spiritual gift generally involves a smaller number of people– often the people who organize the church's overall hospitality program. The book **Widening the Welcome of Your Church** by Fred Bernhard and Steve Clapp describes biblical hospitality in more detail.*

The two years of effort and prayer began to bring results. In the third year of Matt's work with the task force, many members began inviting their friends to participate in church events and to attend worship services. The overall climate of the church became much more welcoming of new people, and a sense of excitement about the future of the congregation began to develop. The twenty year decline in membership was reversed, and the church grew by eighteen percent over the next four years.

Ann's spiritual gifts were hospitality, shepherding, and encouragement. The interaction of those gifts caused her to have especially deep concern for teenage girls in the community whose lives were being limited through pregnancy at too young an age and before marriage. She started talking to social service agencies and school officials in the community and became convinced that churches could be doing more to help teenagers handle their developing sexuality in more positive, Christian-based ways. She got a task force formed in her church, developed some programs to help with the problem, and then persuaded some other congregations to replicate the programs. She had tremendous impact on young people in the community and in the process drew many of them into active church involvement.

Is there a new area of concern to which Christ may be calling you in the life of the church?

Compassion and Witness in Secular Employment

Mike was the manager of a fast food franchise and found it difficult to be as involved as he wanted in his local church. When he took the spiritual gifts assessment, he discovered that his spiritual gifts were especially strong in administration, counseling, and encouragement. He wasn't surprised that he was strong in administration–he used those gifts every day in the fast food business. He was very surprised, however, to find that he had such high scores in counseling and encouragement.

He had no formal training in counseling. His pastor explained to him, however, that counseling as a spiritual gift isn't the same as counseling as a profession. As they visited together, Mike remembered that some of his most satisfying times as a manager had been when he was able to help employees with problems in their personal lives or when he was able to mediate tensions in the workplace.

Most of the time, however, Mike recognized that he felt much too busy to do any counseling at all. He was organizing people and occasionally teaching people, but he had no time to counsel. In fact he knew that many of his younger employees referred to him as "Mad Mike" because he chewed them out so severely when they made mistakes. His older employees knew that his bark was worse than his bite and would in fact complain right back at him.

Then he thought about a teenage girl who had quit the preceding week when he had yelled at her for being ten minutes late the third day in a row. She had looked at him, said "I can't take this," thrown her apron on the floor, and walked out. He had felt a little badly for yelling at her but had also been relieved that she had quit, since he figured she would have to be fired in time anyway.

He asked himself: What kind of attitude is that? If I have gifts in counseling and encouragement, why am I failing to use them in what I do? What if I had talked to her about why she was late and taken a few minutes to understand what was happening in her life? That's what I'd want someone else to do with my son or daughter.

The spiritual gifts process had made Mike more aware of the reality that everyone is a child of God–that everyone has gifts to be used in God's service. Mike realized that he wasn't making the most of his own gifts and that he wasn't doing a good job of seeing those who worked for him as the sons and daughters of God.

The pastor had suggested that everyone could benefit from seeing their secular work as a ministry. Mike began to contemplate what it would mean to see his managerial position as a ministry. He knew he couldn't proselytize people at work, trying to convert them to his own brand of Christianity, but he could sure change how he related to people.

The concept excited him, and he began to make lists of things he could do differently:

- Stopping yelling at people for mistakes, and starting to talk calmly to them.
- Seeking opportunities to learn more about the people who worked for him, and being open to ways in which he could be of help to them.
- Learning to see everyone who came into the restaurant and everyone who worked there as a child of God.
- Teaching his employees to have greater respect for the customers and a stronger desire to help them feel welcome.
- Being ready to help employees with their problems and to encourage them in their lives rather than being annoyed with them.

The changes took time, but Mike was overwhelmed by the results. He started to feel completely different about his work, and he actually saw production improve among all his employees. Morale was much better, and people weren't quitting so frequently. He also found that he had opportunities to talk about the faith with people which he had never considered before. Many people who worked for him were already active in other congregations, and it was fun to talk with them about their faith and their churches. A lot of the younger people weren't active in a church, but they almost all were interested in God and in religious concerns.

What could God be calling you to see differently or do differently in your secular employment? Or could God be calling you to different, more meaningful employment?

Ministry in the Community

As already described, Ann saw a significant need in the community (pregnant teenagers) and involved her church in responding to that need. People may feel called to ministry in the community in a large number of ways, sometimes through the church and sometimes not. For example:

- Evelyn has been a volunteer with the United Way for more than ten years. She doesn't agree with the work of every single organization which receives support from the United Way, but she affirms most of them and believes that it is very important to have a funding agency like the United Way. She sees that work as a direct outgrowth of her faith in Christ and as an important ministry.

- Judy scored high on craftsmanship when she took the spiritual gifts assessment. She started talking to people who worked with the homeless–especially with the director of a shelter which had too little space. She found an abandoned building near the existing shelter, convinced the owner to donate it to the shelter, persuaded suppliers to donate the needed materials, and worked with two friends to remodel the building to provide more room for the homeless.

- George retired five years ago from years working in a factory. Retirement had been boring for him, especially since his wife had continued to work. When he took the spiritual gifts assessment, he was intrigued by how high he scored on encouragement.

He realized that there was no one he was encouraging to do anything and decided to do something about it. He became involved in a Boys and Girls Club in his community and began taking an active interest in several young people, urging them to get more training and education. He also brought three young people into contact with his church's youth pastor which resulted in their becoming part of the church.

* Marge became increasingly aware of the fact that large numbers of young people in the community were being sentenced to a juvenile correctional center. The youth she knew who had been placed there did not improve as a result–in fact, they quickly became far greater behavioral problems than they had been. At first, she didn't know what to do with her concerns and felt inadequate to change things. Then she took a spiritual gifts assessment and found herself scoring very high on administration and leadership. She began to consider the possibility that God was calling her to do something about the juvenile justice system. She became an advocate for youth and organized successful efforts to change policies at the juvenile correctional center.

* Butch and Candy were annoyed by the fact that a single parent who moved next door to them seemed to be having so much trouble supervising her children. The children appeared to be completely on their own for at least two hours every day at the end of school. The oldest was twelve and was supposed to be in charge but couldn't control his

younger brother and sister. Butch and Candy had been thinking about reporting the mother to child welfare for neglecting her children. Then their pastor preached about the need to be open to God's call in our lives and suggested that God sometimes calls us in unexpected ways. They invited their neighbors to have dinner with them and discovered that the mother was working many hours at a low paying job and was deeply concerned about her children. Candy started supervising the children between the time school ended and the time their mother got home, and Butch helped their mother find a better-paying job.

To what need is God calling you in your community? How can you most effectively use your spiritual gifts in the service of others?

Is God Calling You to the Pastoral Ministry?

All of us are involved in ministry, or at least we should be involved in ministry. That's been a recurring theme in this book. The pastoral ministry involves those persons who feel called to give leadership and service to the congregation as a pastor. That can be full-time or part-time, and it may be with or without pay. Certain spiritual gifts, like teaching, prophecy, leadership, evangelism, and administration, are obviously of significant help to those who become pastors. The reality is, however, that one finds tremendous diversity in the spiritual gifts which pastors have. Some persons who score very low on prophecy and teaching nevertheless function very effectively as pastors.

John seemed to have a gift for public speaking and had given the sermon several times when the pastor was on vacation. When their pastor resigned and the church needed an interim, several people mentioned that they sure enjoyed listening to John and that he was actually a better speaker than the last pastor! John wasn't sure about that and also recognized that there was a lot more to being a pastor than giving the sermon.

When other volunteers came forward to accept some of the other responsibilities during the interim, John finally agreed to give the sermons and to help coordinate some of the activities. Since he owned his own business, he had some flexibility in meeting with people who wanted to talk to him.

He didn't accept any pay for the work and at first was praying daily for a permanent pastor to be found in a hurry. Then he began to realize that he was enjoying not only the speaking on Sunday morning but also the work with individuals and committees as people increasingly turned to him for guidance. He seemed to be a natural leader, and he began to hope the church took a long time to find a permanent pastor.

When the church did find a permanent pastor, John decided to take some seminary courses. He had spent a lot of time preparing each sermon, including research in *The Interpreter's Bible* and other references; but he felt that there was a lot more he needed to know about the Bible and theology. As he met people in seminary, he began to accept invitations to fill pulpits for people on vacation or sick.

Then an executive in his denomination asked him to consider being the interim pastor in a church about fifty miles from his business. The distance made that a little difficult for John, but he also found himself delighted with the opportunity. He began to realize that he indeed felt a call to the ministry. He didn't sell his business, but he did decide to become bivocational–something into which he had already drifted through the two interim experiences. He took more seminary courses and completed the formal licensing process for his denomination.

Jim retired after thirty years as a public school teacher and principal. He had always been very active in his church and became even more so in his retirement years. His son, who had moved to a nearby community, called his father on a Saturday night to ask if he would consider speaking in his son's church the next morning, since the pastor had been hospitalized earlier that evening. At first, Jim said that he couldn't possibly do that. His son reminded him of how much he had studied the Bible all his life and of how often he had spoken in the course of his work as a teacher and principal. Jim accepted the invitation.

He felt like he did a poor job speaking the next morning. There hadn't been enough time to prepare, and he had felt that his background was inadequate. Yet people responded positively to him, and he had to admit that he enjoyed the experience. He thought more about his own church and about the incredible work load the pastor had. Was there more he could do to be of help?

Both Jim and his wife had good pensions and good health. Jim began to visit with his own pastor about the possibility of becoming an unpaid assistant. His pastor was very excited by the idea, and they worked out a division of responsibilities. The pastor also developed a reading program to help Jim learn more about church leadership.

Two years later Jim was formally licensed by the denomination, began taking some additional courses, and was named the pastor of a medium-sized congregation. The congregation increased in attendance and in activity under his leadership.

Beth graduated from seminary when she was forty-five years old and began pastoring a small congregation. She had frankly hoped for a larger church, but she quickly fell in love with the members. Then the largest employer in the relatively small community closed a factory, and the unemployment rate went to 30%. The church simply could not continue to pay Beth's full-time salary. Since Beth's husband had a disability and they had two children in college, there was no way they could survive on what the church could afford to pay. Beth initiated the process of searching for a new church but didn't feel good about it. She loved the people and knew they needed her.

As she shared her concerns with the local school administrator who belonged to the church, he mentioned to her that they were going to have a teaching position opening. Beth had taught for years before starting seminary and had continued to teach while attending seminary classes. She realized that with what the teaching position would pay, the provision of the parsonage by the church, and the part-time pay from the church, she and her family could be in better shape financially than they had been while she was pastoring full-time. It would enable her to keep ministering to people who needed her.

Tanya was working on an undergraduate degree in business and was planning to apply for admission to a Masters of Business Administration program. When she learned that her home church was seeking a college student to do youth work the summer between her junior and senior years, she decided to apply for the position. She was delighted when she was accepted.

The pastor of the church had come after Tanya had started college, and Tanya hadn't known her well until beginning the internship. She and the pastor met weekly to brainstorm and set priorities, and Tanya increasingly looked forward to those times of sharing. She began to feel that God might be calling her to the ministry.

When she talked about that with her pastor, the pastor encouraged her and also pointed out that the church needs leaders who have a solid understanding of business. After weeks of prayer, many discussions with the pastor, and a visit to a seminary, Tanya decided to complete both the M.B.A. and a Masters of Divinity. She became one of the most effective pastors in her denomination.

Whatever your gender, age, or stage in life, is it possible that God is calling you to the pastoral ministry? If God is not calling you to that ministry, then to what is God calling you?

More about Spiritual Gifts

The spiritual gifts we possess have implications for our roles in the life of the church and for our secular roles as well. The chart which follows lists examples of church roles and secular roles which seem especially appropriate for persons with particular spiritual gifts.

Spiritual Gift	Church Roles	Secular Roles
prophecy	preaching social action mission work	politics, law, social work, voice of conscience in corporations, editorial writer
teaching	teaching, preaching, worship leadership, youth work, seminary faculty, mentoring, nursery school	teaching in schools or businesses, some types of sales & management, Internet design, medical fields, nursery school
artistic expression	music, drama, worship leadership, creation of art (banners, etc.) for the church, landscaping	music, theater, video production, painting, sculpture, interior design, architecture, floral design, landscaping
intercession	regular prayer for the church & its ministry, prayer group activity, worship leadership	prayer for the needs of the world, living a life of prayer in the midst of a corporate environment
administration	pastoring, chairing groups, business/office work (paid or volunteer), newsletter, stewardship, denominational executive	management at many levels, entrepreneurial work including self-employment, accounting, banking, directing food service or nursing home work
craftsmanship	property maintenance, sets & costumes for drama, outreach through Habitat for Humanity, floral work, emergency disaster response	construction, plumbing, electrical work, running a business in those fields if also gifted in administration, florist, volunteer work building/improving housing

generosity	direct gifts to the church, stewardship education, financial campaigns, discipleship training	consulting or fund-raising for nonprofits (volunteer or paid), banking, gifts to nonprofits
service	property maintenance, kitchen work, office work, child care, youth work, wedding planning, fund-raising, greeter, usher, disaster response	maintenance engineering, food service, office work, child care, youth work, professional wedding planning, fund-raising, law enforcement, retail, nursing
counseling	counseling, teaching youth work, working for greater sensitivity in church groups, crisis counseling, camp counselor	counseling, teaching, youth work, sales, social work, medical fields, human resources, volunteer work in counseling centers
encouragement	caregivers or deacons (depending on church structure), counseling, missions, social action	management, human resources, funeral home, counseling, medical, law enforcement, social work, fitness instructor, coach, teaching
evangelism	pastor, evangelist, caregiving, greeter, usher, outreach to nonmembers	integrate into any kind of work as appropriate, sales, motivational speaker
hospitality	hospitality to visitors & persons in need, voice of conscience to groups, social action, missions, hosting groups	social work, nursing home work, foster parenting, medical, work with the homeless (volunteer or paid), customer service
leadership	pastor, chair of groups, financial campaigns, teaching, denominational executive, religious institution staff	management, politics, entrepreneurial work including self-employment, medicine

The preceding chart contains examples but is certainly not exhaustive of the possibilities. Studying the chart may help you identify:

- Volunteer church roles, at the congregational level or beyond, which you may want to consider.

- The extent to which your gifts may point in the direction of pastoral ministry.

- Volunteer opportunities in the community to which you may be called.

- Secular employment which seems an especially good fit with your spiritual gifts. If you are considering bivocational ministry, these possibilities may be especially helpful. Refer to chapters three and four for more discussion on kinds of secular work which are often complementary to pastoral work.

We encourage you to pray about the spiritual gifts which you have received and the ministries to which God is calling you. Read the Bible, visit with people you trust, and prayerfully seek God's guidance for your life.

*Now the Lord came and stood there, calling
as before, "Samuel, Samuel!" And Samuel
said, "Speak, for your servant is listening."*

1 Samuel 3:10

*Bless the Lord, all his hosts, his ministers
that do his will.*

Psalm 103:21

*The gifts he gave were that some would be
apostles, some prophets, some evangelists,
some pastors and teachers, to equip the
saints for the work of ministry, for building
up the body of Christ, until all of us come
to the unity of the faith and of the knowledge of the Son of God, to maturity, to the
measure of the full stature of Christ.*

Ephesians 4:12-13

*We have gifts that differ according to the
grace given to us: prophecy, in proportion
to faith; ministry in ministering; the teacher
in teaching; the exhorter in exhortation;
the giver in generosity; the leader, in
diligence; the compassionate, in cheerfulness.*

Romans 12:6-8

*As for you, always be sober, endure suffering,
do the work of an evangelist, carry out your
ministry fully.*

2 Timothy 4:5

There are many spiritual gifts. The assessment system in this book measures those which are commonly found, but no system can measure all the gifts our Lord shares.

Appendix–More Spiritual Gifts

The assessment exercise in chapter two deals with the gifts which are commonly found and are used on a regular basis in the ministry of the body of Christ. There are additional gifts which are not so readily measured by any assessment process and which are not as commonly encountered. Some of these, such as the gifts of discernment and of tongues, can be sources of controversy if used unwisely. You may find these short descriptions of interest:

Apostleship: The God-given ability to start churches and supervise their development.

Discernment: The God-given ability to tell the difference between that which is true and that which is false in matters of the church and the faith. [This is not the same as the kind of discernment of God's will that is often sought through a corporate body in decision-making and the calling of people to particular tasks.]

Healing: The God-given ability to be a channel for God's healing power.

Interpretation: The God-given ability to make known the message of one who speaks in tongues.

Tongues: The God-given ability to speak in a language in which one has never been instructed or to speak with an unknown language given by the Spirit (as a kind of prayer language).

Discussion Guide

This guide is provided primarily for those wishing to study this book in a Sunday school class, seminary class, pastor's class, church board, or other setting. Those reading the book as individuals may find it helpful to reflect on the issues raised in this study guide. You can customize the use of this Discussion Guide to fit the needs of your class or group. Enough "extra sessions" have been provided for this to be used as a thirteen week study in place of regular Sunday school curriculum. You can also cover the entire book in six sessions (one per chapter) if you wish. If your group is primarily interested in the spiritual gifts assessment process, then you may want to focus your study on the material for chapters one, two, and six. If bivocational ministry is your primary interest, then focus your study on chapters three, four, and five.

Chapter One Study Guide
What Is Ministry?

1.   Begin by asking the group to brainstorm tasks which they feel are part of ministry (pastoral ministry, individual ministry, or the church's ministry). Write those on chalkboard or newsprint. For example: preaching, counseling, administration, spiritual direction, evangelism, performing marriages, ... Provide paper so people can make their own lists as you write the tasks on chalkboard or newsprint. Then ask members to go through their lists and mark each task with:
   P if only the **pastor** should normally do this task.
   M if only church **members** should normally do this task.
   B if **both** the pastor and church members should normally do this task.
Take hand counts to see how many categorized each item in a particular way. Then talk together about the results: With what items were people not in agreement? Why? Were you surprised at the number of items seen as the responsibility of members or of both members and the pastor? Why, or why not?

2.   Have a volunteer read aloud **1 Corinthians 12:14-26**. Discuss: What does this passage say about the importance of each person to the body of Christ? Ask each person to share which part of the body he or she most strongly identifies with and to share the reason for that selection. For

example: *I identify with the feet because I do so many errands for the church.*

3.   Michael, Laura, and John, as described in the chapter, have three different kinds of ministry. Ask: With which of these three persons did you most strongly identify? Why? What kinds of training do you think are needed for the respective ministries of Michael, Laura, and John? (Chapter five will have more to say on the topic of training for ministry.)

4.   This chapter discusses the concept of "free ministry," in which people serve the church as a team without direct compensation. While that model has been used a lot in smaller churches, it has also been used with some fairly large congregations. Whether this model has been used in your denomination or not, talk about its strengths and weaknesses. What would a church gain from a "free ministry"? What would be lost without a salaried pastor? Are we too dependent on employed staff in the church? Why, or why not?

5.   Close with a prayer of thanksgiving for the ministries of the church.

For an extra session: Invite the pastor or another member of your church staff to meet with your group. Go through the opening exercise with that person and talk about whose responsibility those tasks should be. Ask that person to share the joys and the frustrations of working for the church.

If you are only going to be spending one session on the second chapter, consider asking people to complete the spiritual gifts assessment exercise before class so that you will have more time for discussion.

Chapter Two Study Guide
Gifts for Ministry

Preparation: Consider making extra copies of the spiritual gifts assessment exercise in chapter two which can be given to group members. That way they can complete the exercise in their books and still have a copy to give to a friend or a family member.

1.   Begin by having a volunteer read aloud **1 Corinthians 12:1-11 and 27-31.** (Remember that verses 12-26 were covered in the material for Chapter One.) Discuss: According to verse seven, each person in the body of Christ has at least one spiritual gift. What does this say about the importance of each person to the ministry of the church? When people are inactive in the church, what harm does that do to the church's ministry? Are there areas of your

church's ministry which would benefit from someone coming forward with clear spiritual gifts in that area? In what areas does your church seem to be especially gifted?

2.   Briefly summarize the materials on pages 26-29 on what spiritual gifts *are not* and *are*.

3.   Have group members complete the spiritual gifts assessment exercise.

4.   Divide into pairs or triads to give people opportunity to visit with one another about the results of the spiritual gifts assessment.

5.   Close with a prayer of thanksgiving for the spiritual gifts represented in your class or group.

For an extra session: Assign the biblical passages on page 33 to small groups (or to individuals if your class or group is small), and ask each group or person to prepare a summary for the larger group about what was learned from the passage.   You may wish to further subdivide 1 Corinthians 12–14 because that is so much material.
      Write all of the spiritual gifts on chalkboard or newsprint.   Then ask for a show of hands to determine how many persons had each gift as one of his or her top four.   Which gifts are strongly represented in your group?   Which are not strongly represented?   How is a church affected when some spiritual gifts are underrepresented?   Invite people to share: Did anyone identify a spiritual gift which was a major surprise?   Why?   How do you feel about the work you are currently doing in the church in light of the spiritual gifts exercise?   Does the identification of your spiritual gifts suggest any new call to ministry at your place of work or in the community?   Did any persons have a friend or family member complete an assessment?   If so, what differences, if any, did you notice between your self-assessment and the other person's assessment?

For another extra session: Invite a person to share with your group who is familiar with the spiritual gift of speaking in tongues. This might be a person who actually possesses that gift, or it might be a person who has been present when other people exercised that gift. Talk as a group about that gift and about the other spiritual gifts identified in the Appendix (page 115).

Chapter Three Study Guide
Bivocational Ministry

1. Begin by having a volunteer read aloud **1 Samuel 3:1-10** which describes God's call of Samuel to prophetic activity. Discuss: If God is trying to say something to you in your life, what do you think He is saying? What is He saying to your congregation?

2. Discuss:
    *   Have *you* ever felt called by God to do a particular task, to follow a career call, to establish a relationship, to make other changes in your life. . . . or to dedicate your life to a particular vocation?
    *   Just as Jonah was captured by the whale for not following God's call, has there ever been a time that you felt you did NOT answer God's call? How did you feel, or what did you experience?
    *   What kinds of challenges, highlights, or conflicts did you experience in different areas of your life due to a call (i.e. the call to bivocational ministry causes many to experience an impact on family life)?
    *   Do you feel that God is calling you at this particular moment?

3. **Suppose you inherited 10 million dollars!!** How would this single event change your life? How would it change your outlook and attitude about work? About other people? How would it affect your involvement in the church? Your relationship with God?

4. Share this background: *In the bivocational study, about 81% of survey respondents were in favor of encouraging bivocational ministry. Only 55% support the idea of encouraging it among seminary students. A higher percentage supported encouraging older members to become ministers.* Discuss:
    *   Are you in favor of bivocational ministry within your denomination as a whole?
    *   Would you be open to having a bivocational minister serve *your own congregation*? (If one is already doing so, then you can discuss the strengths and weaknesses of that arrangement for your church.)
    *   Share at least two strengths and two weaknesses of bivocational ministry.
    *   What do you think of encouraging seminary students to think of other options for employment? Of encouraging older members of the church to become pastors? Share the reasons for your responses.

5. Close with a prayer thanking God for the many forms that ministry takes.

For an extra session: Focus your session around three major questions:
1. What would your "ideal minister" be like? (Do NOT list any names.) What qualities does he or she possess? How involved is the minister with the congregation? With the community? What tasks does the minister perform? What are the major areas of emphasis in sermons?
2. What is YOUR ministry? Name at least two ways that you are a "minister" within the church and two ways that you minister to others outside of your immediate congregation.
3. What is your CONGREGATION'S ministry? Name at least three ways you believe your congregation has a particular "mission" to fulfill.

Chapter Four Study Guide
Balancing Secular Work and Ministry

1. Begin by sharing these words from **2 Timothy 4:5**: *As for you, always be sober, endure suffering, do the work of an evangelist, carry out your ministry fully.* Discuss: How have you handled the stresses and strains of your life? How has it affected your relationships with God, family, friends, and other members of your church?

2. Share this information: *According to the survey completed by bivocational pastors, many ministers experience high levels of stress, burnout, and frustration due to lack of time with family and friends, failure to live up to the expectations of others, and feeling like one is serving "two masters."* Discuss:
   - Examine your own moments of greatest stress. What are the major causes of stress in your life?
   - How involved are you with the life of the church? Have you felt "stressed" from taking caring of church "business"? Why, or why not?
   - How does your own stress impact others in the church? Do you feel alienated from God, others, and even yourself?
   - Why do people experience burnout in church involvement? List at least three reasons and discuss them with others in the group (i.e., lack of appreciation, other things going on in one's life, conflicts with other members, lack of time, personal or family health, etc.).

3. Put a chart like the one which follows on chalkboard or newsprint. Work as a group to complete the chart. What are the ideal expectations? What is reality? Compare the two categories, and discuss the ramifications for the life and growth of the church.

	IDEAL EXPECTATIONS	REALITY
Your ministry		
Your pastor's ministry		
Your church's ministry		

4. Talk about these concerns:
   *   How do you balance expectations between ideal and actual situations?
   *   If fully in control of your life, how much time would you spend on each task? For example: sleeping, working, family activities, church activities, community involvement, self-improvement, personal devotions, physical exercise, ...
   *   What is a fair expectation for the amount of time the minister spends with the congregation? What is a fair expectation for the time the minister spends working outside of the congregation?
   *   Imagine yourself in the role of pastor to your church. What things would you do differently from the present pastor? What would be the same? What are the negative and positive experiences of being a pastor to your church?
   *   Imagine being a bivocational minister. What new stresses and/or benefits would be added? What kind of support would you desire as a bivocational minister (i.e., financial, emotional, volunteer, etc.)? How does that differ from what a full-time minister needs if that person does not have additional employment?

5. Close with a prayer seeking God's help with the stress at work in your own life and in the life of the church.

For an extra session: Invite your pastor or another member of the church staff to meet with the group and talk about the pressures of working for the church. Identify ways that your church could be more supportive of its staff, whether the staff is paid or unpaid. Then talk about ways that the congregation can help volunteers avoid burnout from their work in the church.

Chapter Five Study Guide
The Need for Trained Ministers

1. Begin by giving members time to silently read the **second chapter of Acts**. Then discuss:
    *   What cultural and other religious practices were brought into the early Christian church which were unacceptable to the apostles? What danger did that present to the church?
    *   Consider ways in which our culture also puts pressure upon the church to accept practices and/or doctrines which are not found in the teachings of Jesus. How does your congregation hold itself accountable to the teachings of Christ? What beliefs and practices generally assumed to be Christian may in fact not be?

2. What should be required of pastors and teachers to become competent leaders in the church? Make a list on chalkboard or newsprint. What training does your congregation expect pastors and teachers to receive before serving as leaders?

3. Focus discussion on the impact of change:
    *   How has your community changed since 1960? Make a list and discuss ways in which those changes have impacted your church and others in the area (for example: schools, shopping centers, employment, transportation, etc.).
    *   How have you personally felt about those changes? Where do you generally anticipate change in your life and how do you prepare for it? Where do you resist change, and why?
    *   How did Jesus prepare for change in his life? How did he prepare the disciples for change? Are these ways for dealing with change, which Jesus taught, the same as those we use in the church today?

4. Now focus discussion on the final part of the chapter:
    *   Make a list of leadership development opportunities available to leaders in your congregation. How many of those are feasible for persons to participate in? Which are impossible, and why? What opportunities are needed which are not available?
    *   When and where do the fundamental issues of the Christian faith get discussed in your church, and who participates?
    *   About what percentage of your congregation do you believe could describe your denomination's ministry training program? Do you believe most people who attend your congregation see the denomination as a vital way to promote and teach the Christian faith?

- What obstacles do small congregations have in developing a teaching ministry? What strengths to they have?
- Given today's lifestyle for families, what do you believe would be the best way to train leaders and teach the Christian Faith?
- What are the strengths of a congregationally based ministry training program, such as Education For a Shared Ministry (EFSM)?

5. Close with a prayer, giving thanks for strong leadership in the church.

For an extra session: Invite a person who has knowledge of the ministerial training programs in your denomination to visit with your group. This might be a pastor, a seminary student, a seminary faculty member, or a person from your regional judicatory.

Chapter Six Study Guide
What Is Your Ministry?

1.   Begin by having a volunteer read aloud **Philippians 1:3–5**. Discuss: How do we all share in the gospel? What differences are there in the ways that these persons share in the gospel: full-time clergy? bivocational clergy? active members of the church? people who believe in Christ but are not part of a local church?

2.   Consider the discussion of ways to encourage and support professional clergy in chapter six. Brainstorm your own list of things members of the class or group can do to support and encourage local church and denominational staff.

3.   Focus attention on the part of this chapter which discusses making the most of your spiritual gifts within the life of the church. Ask group members: Are there new ministries to which you feel called in the life of our church as a result of this study? If so, what are they? What changes, if any, do you think our congregation as a whole should make?

4.   If you are participating in this study as a class or group in a local church, most of the persons in your group probably earn their living through secular employment. Generate a list of ideas about ways in which spiritual gifts can affect how we handle secular employment. Discuss: Does anyone in the group feel a calling to a different kind of employment as a result of this study? If so, what and why? What ways have you identified for better utilizing your spiritual gifts at your place of work or in your daily life in the community?

5.   Give each person in the group a piece of paper and these instructions: *Think of someone in your congregation who you believe would be a good pastor, and write his or her name on a piece of paper. Also list on the paper two or three reasons why this person would be an effective minister.*

Put the names into a bowl, so people do not have to be identified with the name written down. Have a group member read off each name. Discuss as a group the reasons why each person named would be a good candidate for ministry (before reading aloud the reasons listed on the paper).

How should the congregation go about calling candidates for a ministry role in the church? What kind of support would you provide for a candidate going through the ministerial training process?

6.   Share a prayer seeking God's guidance in determining the kind of ministry to which each group member is called.

For an extra session: Invite five people from a variety of occupations to visit with the group about the way they see their faith connected to their secular employment.

Christian Community, the publisher of this resource, offers a variety of materials to help congregations with church growth, biblical hospitality, stewardship education, fund-raising, and worship. Some of those are described on the following pages. Contact us for a free catalog:

Christian Community
6404 S. Calhoun Street
Fort Wayne, Indiana 46807
419-872-7448
E-mail: DadofTia@aol.com

The Brethren Academy for Ministerial Leadership is committed to providing training and encouragement for ministry. The Academy offers two approaches to ministerial training which are described on pages 84-88 of this book. For further information, contact:

The Brethren Academy
Bethany Theological Seminary
615 National Road West
Richmond, Indiana 47374
1-800-287-8822

Christian Community Ministry Resources

If you found this book of interest, you may also want to consider the following publications from Christian Community:

Creating Quality in Ministry by Steve Clapp and Cindy Hollenberg Snider. "Quality" has become a popular buzz word in secular and religious circles, but what does it mean when applied to the ministry of the congregation? This book offers practical strategies for sharpening the focus and enhancing the impact of local church ministry. Chapters cover concerns such as:

- Understanding Quality
- What Quality Means in the Church
- Finding, Preparing, and Reinforcing Volunteer Leadership
- Quality in Christian Education
- Organizing Time and Work
- Gaining Healthy Feedback
- Quality in Pastoral Care
- Quality in Traditional Worship
- Quality in Contemporary Worship

Overcoming Barriers to Church Growth by Steve Clapp. Let's face it– twenty years of church growth programs, promotions, rallies, books, videos, conferences, and resolutions haven't reversed the trend of decline in many mainline Protestant churches. In *Overcoming Barriers to Church Growth,* Steve Clapp goes beyond his classic book *Plain Talk about Church Growth* to confront the attitudes and barriers to growth which congregational leaders face. Among other things, you'll learn:

- The truth about the relationship between demographics and growth.
- Why ministerial style is directly related to growth.
- How to overcome low congregational self-esteem.
- How to overcome a volunteer shortage, inadequate visitor follow-up, and difficult new member assimilation.

Judy Turner, executive with the Disciples of Christ, said: "Finally, a book on church growth that recognizes the reality that demographics do make it difficult for churches to grow. Yet any congregation can find clear direction and hope for a faithful future through this book."

Reaching Out through Christian Education by Steve Clapp and Jerry O. Cook. In this landmark book, Steve and Jerry draw on experiences in local churches across North America to give you the handles you need to revitalize your church's educational program and in the process the whole congregation. You'll discover:

- Why you should add leaders before adding students.
- Strategies to reactivate inactives and to KEEP people coming.
- The right and wrong ways to use attendance & participation awards.
- How to reach the divorced, the handicapped, and many others the church too often misses.
- How to teach people to share their faith and reach out.

Herb Miller, of **Net Results**, called this "an excellent resource."

Reaching the Forgotten by Steve Clapp, Julie Seibert Berman, Pat Helman, & Cindy Hollenberg Snider. Many strategies for church growth urge members to reach out primarily to people like themselves. While those strategies have an important place and build on our natural relationships in the community, they also can cause us to overlook whole categories of persons. This cutting edge book offers realistic strategies for reaching out to:
- Single parents and their children.
- The poor.
- People with alcohol and other drug addictions.
- Persons with terminal illness and those who care for them.
- Persons who have been to prison and their families.
- Victims of crime.

Excerpts from this book were featured on the **LIVE IT!** website of **Religion Today.**

The Desires of Your Heart–Financial Giving and the Spiritual Life by Holly Carcione, Steve Clapp, Kristen Leverton, and Angela Zimmerman. This book shares the results of our research on stewardship and the spiritual life in the form of practical strategies which any church can use to improve its financial base. The chapters build on the ten ways to increase giving that were identified in the study, providing specific ways to implement change in the congregation. This book can help you identify the dynamics at work in your congregation in the area of stewardship and will help you develop an overall strategy to improve giving while deepening the spiritual life. Loren Mead, founder of the **Alban Institute**, said: "This is a very practical book which should produce excellent results for congregations which are facing stewardship challenges realistically. This is an understandable framework for leaders who want their congregation to be healthier as a sound institution, but it also pushes beyond the financial to the spiritual dimension of financial health."

Widening the Welcome of Your Church by Fred Bernhard and Steve Clapp. Pastor Fred Bernhard, convinced that hospitality is an essential part of the Gospel, developed a comprehensive model of a welcoming congregation which has had dramatic impact. His congregation, located in rural Ohio, experienced a 19% increase in worship attendance and a 36% increase in Sunday school attendance in the first three months using this model–and the growth has continued. Steve Clapp studied the impact of similar strategies in other congregations, and they combined their experience to produce this highly motivational and practical book. A study guide, originally a separate publication, is now part of this powerful resource.

Hospitality and the Vital Church Video. This short video is a companion to *Widening the Welcome* and takes you inside Fred's church to experience the impact of hospitality on the life of the congregation. An excellent introduction to class, group, or church-wide study of this resource.

Sharing Living Water by Steve Clapp and Sam Detwiler. While most church members readily agree that they should share their faith with others and invite them to church, many are not comfortable doing so. This practical, easy-to-understand book helps people identify:
- The natural connecting points which give opportunities to share their faith or invite others to church without being manipulative.
- How to express their faith and the importance of the church in their own words rather than by a formula.
- Strategies to effectively assimilate visitors into the life of the congregation.

Steve and Sam also collaborated on a book called *Peer Evangelism*, about which **Presbyterian Youth Leader** wrote: "an excellent resource for faith-sharing."

Alternatives for Worship by Cindy Hollenberg Snider and Steve Clapp. This book contains twenty ready-to-use, non-traditional worship services. The resource is in a convenient loose-leaf notebook format–ideal for removing pages to reproduce since permission to photocopy is included!

Services use an assortment of media, including drama, video clips, reader's theater, storytelling, guided meditation, group sharing, and music to communicate the Gospel. Worship themes include:
- **Vegetarian Fair**: Using a drama called "Help! My Daughter's a Vegetarian," this service calls attention to the unequal distribution of global resources, God's call to care for creation, and the luxuries we take for granted.
- **The Titanic–When Dreams Die**: Using a clip from the video blockbuster, this service helps people deal with dreams and hopes that are destroyed and shows how to experience God's vision for the future.

Each service includes an order of worship; the full text of prayers, readings, dramas, etc.; guidance for handling video clips and other special arrangements.

The Alternative Worship Primer by Cindy Hollenberg Snider. This companion booklet to *Alternatives for Worship* is arranged in question-and-answer format to help churches make decisions about and interpret alternative worship. Questions answered in this resource include:
- Why do people want alternative worship experiences?
- How can we determine if there is a need for an alternative service?
- How can we involve enough people to ensure success?
- How can we win approval from people who are happier with traditional worship?
- Where can we find music and musicians?
- How can we generate the funding for such a service?